THE BASICS OF READERS' ADVISORY WORK

THE BASICS OF READERS' ADVISORY WORK

RAY PRYTHERCH

CLIVE BINGLEY LONDON

© Ray Prytherch and Jean Barthel 1988

Published by
Clive Bingley Limited
7 Ridgmount Street
London WC1E 7AE

First published 1988

British Library Cataloguing in Publication Data

Prytherch, R. J.
    The basics of readers' advisory work.
    1. Counselling — Great Britain
    2. Community information services —
    Great Britain
    I. Title
    361'.06   HV245

ISBN 0-85157-389-4

Typeset in 11/12 pt Baskerville by Style Photosetting, Tunbridge Wells, Kent.
Printed and made in England by Redwood Burn Ltd, Trowbridge, Wiltshire.

Contents

Preface

The initiative for this book came originally from the Publishers. Jean Barthel of the Leeds Polytechnic Department of Library and Information Studies was approached to write the volume, and began work. Over several months she collected a considerable quantity of material and made many notes, and from time to time invited my advice and assistance.

Eventually, because of other pressures, she felt unable to continue work on it. I had become convinced that a book on this topic was long overdue and would be a valuable contribution to the professional literature, and in consultation with the Publishers it was agreed that I would write the volume using the notes and other materials already assembled.

As with other volumes in this series, the approach is at an introductory level, and should be suitable reading for all grades of library staff in contact with readers. The emphasis is on a common-sense, practical approach, and there is deliberately no complex analysis of problems.

Readers' advisory work is taken in its broadest context: not simply helping readers with enquiries, but organizing library and information department services in such a way that their staff, premises and stock offer maximum appeal and helpfulness to the greatest number of potential users.

Many colleagues, individually and on behalf of their services, have offered ideas and specimen materials for this volume; I am very pleased to express my grateful acknowledgement of their help.

Ray Prytherch
February 1987

Chapter One

Introduction

Readers' advisory work is a neglected aspect of librarianship; the topic is mentioned in many books, but generally only in passing and without emphasis, and it is many years since substantial works appeared. In the United Kingdom the manuals by Collison (1965) and Hepworth (1951) remain the only two important titles, and inevitably the passage of time and the changing emphasis of librarianship have made them less appropriate than they were, and copies are now not so easy to locate in any case.

The lack of recent literature on readers' advisory work can probably be attributed to two causes: firstly it is so general a subject that some librarians simply overlook it — maybe they feel that anyone who works in a library wants to help readers and so should be left to get on with it as it seems a natural instinctive task. It is true that staff attitudes and individual personalities are essential components of successful work, but we could not accept that so vital an area of communication between staff and readers should be left to chance and common sense. There is no beginning to readers' advisory work, and no end — it is relevant to every transaction in every library — but its formless nature should not prevent a serious examination of what it consists of, and how we can train staff to make a better job of it.

The second difficulty that this topic faces is the competition for our attention from the 'new' aspects of work in libraries. There is no shortage of materials about audio-visual materials, certainly an abundance about the value of computers in libraries; public relations has become an important aspect, as have staff-training, community information and many others. Smaller, simpler subject areas can be analysed, their problems solved, solutions offered, techniques explained, equipment evaluated; but a complex topic like readers' advisory work

cannot be so easily analysed, the problems cannot be fully
solved, there are no fool-proof solutions. Techniques can,
however, be readily acquired, and no equipment is needed. It is
not an easy topic to discuss in a book − all problems, few
solutions, no expensive hardware, and probably no obvious
success at the end of the day.

Although it is not a glamorous subject, readers' advisory work
depends on an extremely expensive component of library
operating costs, and therefore should receive careful attention
and efficient management. If we consider the various costs to be
met in running a library, there are three principal areas of
expenditure: firstly the costs of the building and furniture and
their operation (heating, lighting, insurance, cleaning and
similar charges), secondly the cost of providing the stock −
books, periodicals, audio-visual materials, computer software
etc. − and thirdly the cost of staffing the library to run the
service. It is the third area of cost that concerns us at present.

Frequently we shall find that the costs of the library's premises
are difficult to quantify; except in cases where a new, separate
building has been provided, libraries may be located in shared
premises, for example a library in a school or college, or be
housed in older premises which have been fully paid for over the
years and thus involve no recurrent capital costs or debt charges.
Thus the strict day-to-day costs of a library service, whilst
involving some maintenance charges and administrative costs −
telephone and stationery for instance − are fundamentally a
matter of stock and staff. Much attention is paid to the
acquisition of stock and its physical handling: typically
librarians will read reviews extensively, visit library suppliers and
specialist booksellers, and hold internal meetings to decide what
stock to obtain. In addition the processing of that stock will be
efficiently handled, often by competitive services from library
suppliers, and the record-keeping necessary − cataloguing,
classification, lending operations − will probably be handled by
automated means, which are again expensive but can be
justified by efficiency.

Yet in most library services the costs of the stock will be only
20%−40% of the operating costs; the remainder of the
continuing running costs will be taken up in paying staff to
operate the service. Thus 50% at a minimum will be staff costs,
and in most libraries a figure of 60%−70% is a more realistic
breakdown of the day-to-day costs.

Staff are therefore the most expensive component in a library's costs. To take some simple examples, in a school library a person to run the service might be paid £6,000 per year and be allowed £3,000 for purchase of stock (all figures appropriate to 1987 salary scales); in a small industrial or commercial information unit a staff member working alone might receive £7,000 per year, with £2,000 for stock and another £2,000 for on-line services. In both these cases costs of premises and administration would be subsumed into the budget of the parent organization. For public libraries, long opening hours may mean a large number of part-time staff, and the general ratios that we have seen above will also apply.

The high costs of staff must therefore necessitate careful and efficient use of this resource, but it it quite common to find that this is not so. In many authorities staff are still recruited by haphazard means, or come into employment 'preselected' by various Government schemes to lower unemployment rates. In industrial contexts, recruitment methods are usually 'harder', but personnel officers may have very little experience of job requirements in the information unit. It is a widespread concern about the possible poor image of library assistant staff that has contributed to the growth of organized staff training schemes. There must now be very few public authorities indeed that fail to provide attractive schemes for all new staff, usually designed to give an overview of the whole service. These schemes are obviously vital to a good service and should be encouraged by all means.

The problem from our present viewpoint is that staff are recruited and trained in a general sense, perhaps by a central personnel office, and library stock is bought, processed and put on shelves, both as separate operations. It is more likely than not that the staff in any service point have received no direct, relevant training to enable them to learn which books they have in their library, what those books contain, what else is needed to enable users to find what they want, to trace books, videos, recordings they would like to try, nor received any appropriate information on how to make the stock attractive to users and non-users; in other words it is still commonly seen as sufficient to place the stock on the shelves, leave users who choose to enter free to select whatever they can find, and allow the staff simply to operate the lending procedures and keep the place tidy. But surely this is now inadequate: it cannot be good sense to spend on both parts of the service and not co-ordinate them to produce efficient exploitation of both.

Over the last decade library services in the public sector have seen two major policy lines: positively there has been the move to shift the emphasis of the service to the user i.e. the whole weight of the operation must be geared to the best advantage of the users, not to the benefit of the employees or the delight of booksellers; secondly and more negatively has been the pressure to reduce spending which has resulted too often in reduced opening hours or closure of some service points. Library authorities have generally realized that the best response to the latter constraint has been to concentrate on the more successful achievement of the first demand: standards can be seen to be maintained if user needs can be analysed and then targeted. This also coincides with local government thinking and provides the library with a share of political goodwill.

Serving the user is exactly what readers' advisory work is all about; although some users may be content to walk into a library, browse until they find something that appeals, and borrow it, these people must be in a minority. In some service points it may appear that this is all that seems to be needed, but it must be remembered that if a public library has 25% of the local population using its services it is meeting the national average. 75% of the population find public libraries unattractive and irrelevant, and this is a dangerous ratio in a local government service. Universities, polytechnics, colleges and schools are often appalled by the low level some students and pupils make of the services provided, often scarcely ever entering the building; steps are being taken in this field to make learning more student-centred, a more active process that implies greater individual use of resources. Non-use is a common problem; community advice services go to great lengths to ensure maximum local awareness of their existence; many libraries feel that if they were more 'attractive' they would carry greater local weight and have better funding. It may be argued that old or shabby premises and tatty stock contribute to the image, but fundamentally we might suspect it is the staff — the greatest resource. Even new, attractive buildings with abundant stock in good condition, a wide range of videos, picture-lending schemes, and provision of software and micros, can still be repellent places if the staff are abrupt and unhelpful; on the other hand, genuinely courteous and knowledgeable staff can transform dowdy premises and unpromising stock into a service that meets community needs and merits local praise. In between these two extremes lie all mixes of the good and the bad; maybe this book can help to shift the mood of any kind of library service towards a greater helpfulness to users on the part of every member of the service. Basically this can be achieved at low financial cost, on the premises, without outside help; its results should be a greater satisfaction on the part of the users, satisfaction from the staff with a more competent and fulfilling job, and satisfaction from the parent organization or local authority that a good-quality, cost-effective service is being provided and generating local goodwill.

The purpose of this book is therefore to explore the features that comprise readers' advisory work, and to suggest the ways in which staff can become acquainted with sound methods of practice to achieve a better standard in this area of work.

This book is aimed at people working in smaller types of libraries or information units. Such libraries may be based in schools, sixth-form colleges, or in colleges of further education, where one would hope that the principal member of staff would be professionally qualified although this is far from universally true; or they may be public library service points — full-time or part-time branches, or mobile services — where a young professional librarian or an experienced non-professional member of staff may be in charge of the service; or they may be information units, possibly under national or local government sponsorship — such as Tourist Information Services, Community Health Councils, Development Corporations, Careers Services — or in the voluntary sector, such as Citizens' Advice Bureaux, literacy-scheme organizations, etc.

All such libraries will be small in terms of their stock and the number of staff available, they will probably have only limited financial resources, and their available reference material will be confined to a core of basic items. The staff in such libraries will be a mix of professional and non-professional people, but the more numerous category will be non-qualified library assistant staff, some of whom may be experienced members of staff on supervisory grades. The audience for this book is therefore library assistants and young professional staff in any type of smaller service where stock is limited.

In larger libraries — universities, polytechnics or public library central or major district headquarters — we should expect to find a very wide range of specialist stock, specialized services, and a good proportion of qualified and experienced staff. Training facilities should be well developed, and features such as displays and publicity should be in the hands of appropriately able staff. This volume is expressly not seeking to explore reference materials in great depth, nor to suggest advanced training in communication skills; even so, we might expect library assistants in any context to find some valuable information here.

This book will examine a series of key topics that seem to make up readers' advisory work in its widest sense, and the intention in each chapter will be to define exactly what the topic comprises, to show the problems that could arise from poor standards of work, to suggest ways of improving practices – and here there may be appropriate examples of training materials that might be adapted to suit the local context and where possible, specimens of good publicity will be reproduced to demonstrate what can be achieved, which may spur further ideas for similar initiatives locally.

The first topic to be covered will be the basic strategy for making a library accessible, attractive and usable; in any type of public service the location of premises is important, whether as a separate building in the community, or as a service in a larger organization. Potential users must be able to find the library, they must find it available at suitable times, and it must be accessible for disabled users. Once inside, the user must be guided to essential points and to the layout of the stock; in some services it will be appropriate to arrange programmes of user education to enable people to make more effective use of the service.

The second basic topic is the means of finding out who the users are; this may seem easy in a school or college, but in fact can be quite complex, and in a public library context, or a Citizens' Advice Bureau, or a prison library, the range of people who may use the service, their needs and expectations, will need great energy and application to discover. In every case, working out the likely pattern of user needs will enable the service to target its resouces to those areas most likely to be in demand.

The fourth chapter will look at the types of questions people may ask in a library or information unit; it is possible to have a strategy for any request, although in some cases this may be a procedure for referring the user to a more specialist service point. A wide range of general questions can be answered from a very modest range of reference books. The chapter will consider the strategies required, and will itemize a number of essential works that most libraries should aim to provide and that all staff should be trained to use efficiently.

Following this, chapter 5 will look at some of the more community-based types of information needed to help people in aspects of their day-to-day life. The types of information will probably not be available in printed books − it will have to be collected by the library's staff, and they may be the key link, and possibly the only link in passing on the information to the people who need it.

The sixth chapter will consider how to store and organize materials; much information will be in the form of leaflets, handouts, publicity releases, or material gathered by the library in correspondence or by telephone. Obviously to have an efficient use of resources it must be possible for all staff to know what information is available and to be able to find it again to answer similar questions in the future. The means of doing this by manual methods or by using a simple micro-computer will be discussed, and routines suggested for regular updating.

It is important that users and would-be users should know what services are being offered by their library, what hours it is open, how to join, how to find out what new books are available. Publicity and public relations are now recognized to be vital to the success and survival of all types of libraries; chapter 7 will examine the ways in which they can be cheaply and simply achieved.

Throughout the chapters, the importance of good staff training will be implicit, and the essential component of positive, helpful staff attitudes; in chapter 8 these two themes will be more fully developed. No amount of sound practice as such will succeed if the 'image' of the staff is seen to be less than helpful; this is a pervasive point, and is the key to the whole field of readers' advisory work.

In the final chapter, the major points made throughout the book will be summarized, and conclusions drawn about the actual nature of our topic and the simplicity of the means by which a better level of service can so readily be offered to users.

Chapter Two

First catch your reader

Location

An employee of an organization is the person least able to see the premises in which they work with the eyes of an outsider. After all, if you work in a building, you will know where the entrance is, where the toilets are, on which floor the children's books are kept, and the hours you open.

Readers' advisory work starts outside the library; if you were a stranger what would you be able to find out about your library? If you work in a public branch library, are your premises marked on local street maps, are there signposts to direct those who are not certain where you are? If your base is a mobile library, how do people find out where and when you stop? Remember that 75% of the population do *not* use public libraries, and while determined people might ask the way, most prefer to see directions provided, and it is a courtesy to help them. Anyway, good signposting is good business; retail shops use large neon-lit signs for their names, have distinctive logos and advertise widely — their objective is to keep potential customers aware of their existence and to publicize their location to attract more trade. With the co-operation of the local authority planning department and at small cost public libraries can be 'advertised' on signposts and included on local maps and plans.

In some types of information units the problems of locating the service are just as acute; housing information centres, or consumer protection agencies for example, may well be sited in local government buildings where car parks and landscaping, or just sheer size, may prevent ready pinpointing of just where one needs to be.

In schools and colleges this is not such a problem; after an initial period of chaos new pupils or students find their way about. However, in schools maybe new pupils do not visit the library frequently and their ability to remember its location may not be reliable for several weeks. Slower pupils may need the encouragement of good directional signs to help them pinpoint landmarks in a large confusing building. The library may take advantage of the laxity of other facilities and become the one place that pupils can easily find; they are more likely to go in feeling welcomed. College libraries have part-time students who may visit only once a week, or students on short courses who are at the college for only a few days; clearly it is essential that such students having only limited time for library use should be able to reach the library without wasting time in searching. Lack of clear directions will make them uncomfortable, and may deter them from bothering to find the library at all. It is poor strategy to be mentioned in post-course evaluations only for negative points — 'couldn't find the library'.

It is simpler of course to advertise the library's location if it is in a good position. Public libraries get more custom if they are sited in shopping precincts, or grouped with other amenities that receive heavy public use. Splendid new buildings just outside main shopping streets need so much more effort to publicize than less grand premises right in the middle of things. Libraries in schools and colleges and industrial or advisory information units are also much helped by a central location in the organization, maybe just inside the main entrance or another point where there is much passing 'traffic' that may call in, and a separate journey or long detour is not necessary. Here again, location close to other facilities that many people need to use can be an advantage — next to the photocopying room, or opposite the cafeteria maybe. However, the location of a library is not negotiable, it is sited where it is, and if that location is poor, it means extra effort on directional signposting.

Publicity

Getting people into the library can be further promoted by simple publicity; the whole question of publicity and public relations will be the subject of chapter 7, and it will be enough here to comment on some basic methods.

Publicity leaflets, posters or bookmarks, should be simple, clearly written, contain only essential information, and must always carry the vital locational points — address, telephone number and preferably a map. They may be general introductions (Figure 2.1) or they may specify some particular aspect of the service (for example Figure 2.2) or they may be produced to coincide with the opening of new premises (Figure 2.3). Eye-catching, simple styles can be particularly appealing to children, young adults, and members of the community who find written English difficult (for example Figure 2.4).

It can be especially useful for individual libraries and information units to get together with others to create joint publicity for services which are similar and which will appeal to a similar clientele (e.g. Figure 2.5). Distribution of such publicity can be arranged via schools, colleges, further education classes, made available in community centres, doctors' waiting rooms, post offices, and maybe handed out on a busy Saturday morning in a local supermarket or distributed with local freesheet newspapers or via ordinary newspaper deliveries. A small fee may be charged, but publicity may get into homes that would otherwise never think of using a library.

Access
Access to library premises should also be easy and inviting. It is helpful if car-parking space is available close by, and care needs to be taken for people who use other forms of transport: provision of rails for chaining up bicycles, space to park prams and pushchairs.

For most purposes, single-floor, ground-level premises will be preferable; these are obviously easier for young children and the elderly, and it is a legal obligation to remember the needs of the disabled. Wide, level entrances, or the provision of broad, shallow ramps will be essential; partial solutions using rear entrances or goods lifts are better than nothing for wheelchair patrons, but are very far from ideal.

Information units will need to cater for regular types of user: if young children are often brought in by their parents, then facilities for them to play will be useful; services for elderly people will need to overcome steep steps or heavy doors. College libraries must also make provision for access by disabled students, and many retired people also attend various courses, and may find regular climbing of stairs a nuisance.

Opening hours
However accessible premises are in a physical sense, patrons also need to find them open at convenient times. No amount of effort

MAKING THE MOST OF YOUR LIBRARY

A GUIDE TO KIRKLEES LIBRARY SERVICE

KIRKLEES LIBRARIES

How do I join the Library?

Easily – if you work, live, or study in the Kirklees area you may join any of our libraries. Some form of identification showing name and address should be produced when you apply – then it's just a matter of completing a simple form, and you become a member for life. Children are encouraged to join and there is no lower age limit.

How much does it cost?

It costs nothing to join the library, or to borrow books. Some charges are made for certain special services – see separate leaflets.

How many books can I borrow?

Adults may borrow up to ten books at a time, children may take out up to five books. In libraries where a computer system is in use you will be given one ticket which you use to borrow all your books, and you need this ticket with you everytime you come to borrow books. Try not to lose it – we make a charge of £1 for a replacement. In other libraries a separate ticket is needed for every book you borrow, so you may have a maximum of ten. No charge is made to replace one of these tickets should you lose one.

Can I use any library in Kirklees?

Once you are a member you may use any library in Kirklees, and books borrowed from one place may be returned to any other of our libraries.

How long can I keep my books? Do I have to pay fines if I keep them too long?

You may keep books for up to four weeks – the date due back will be stamped on them. After that period fines are payable, including a separate charge if we have to send a reminder to you. Children and Senior Citizens are exempt from fines.

If I haven't finished my books when they are due back, can I keep them longer?

You may renew the loan for a further four weeks, provided the books are not wanted by someone else. Just call in, telephone, or write, giving the date due back, and the name digit number on the barred strip just below the date label, and the title of the book. If you are writing please give your name and address too.

What happens if I loose or damage a book?

When you borrow a book you become responsible for it. If you lose or seriously damage a book you will be asked to pay the full replacement cost.

The book I want isn't on the library shelves, can you get it for me?

You may request any book, whether or not it is in our stock, and we will do our very best to get it for you. We make a small charge for this.

Do you have sets of music and plays?

Yes – please ask us about this service.

Do you have any books in foreign languages?

Yes, selections of books in major European languages are kept at our larger libraries and changed at regular intervals.

Do you have any Asian language books?

Yes, many of our libraries have selections of Asian language books.

Can I borrow records and cassettes?

Many of our libraries do offer this service, a range of records and cassettes is available, classical and pop, music, talking books, cas... children, language courses and general info... cassettes. The Beatles or Beethoven, Shake... Status Quo, we should have something... are an adult member of the libra... records and cassettes using your... ticket. The loan period is four we... small charge is made. Registere... handicapped people are exempt... Senior Citizens may... A maximum of five r... borrowed at one tim...

Can I borrow c... home?

Attractive... well as c... of our lar... up to 12... this serv...

Fig. 2.1

Right from the earliest age, children benefit from coming into contact with books. Sheffield children's library services provide a convenient and free source of selected children's books for all ages. There are board books for babies, picturebooks, easy readers for children starting to read for themselves, fiction for the middle years and novels for young adults. We have a large range of non-fiction, and there are information books to help with school work as well as books about leisuretime hobbies.

Children's books are provided in the Central Children's Library, branch libraries and mobile libraries throughout the city, and you are welcome to bring your child along to any of them.

How to join

Ask at your library for a child's joining form. The form will need a parent's or guardian's signature. When it is completed, take the form back to the library and you will be given your ticket(s). Children can borrow up to five books at a time, and there is no lower age limit for joining. Children are not charged fines for overdue books, although we would appreciate it if you could encourage them to renew books if they want them for longer than three weeks!

Much more than books

Many junior libraries have storyhours and other special children's activities. These sessions are free, and staff at the library can give you further details.

The free children's magazine "Choice" is produced regularly, and special booklists are often available for reading guidance. We take a variety of popular magazines for children to read in the library.

During the summer, there are special events for children including a Summer Fun Quiz. In October, National Children's Book Week is the focus for yet more competitions and entertainment.

Special services

Playgroup leaders can borrow up to twenty books by special arrangement with their library. The Central Children's Library lends books to state nurseries which are funded by Family and Community Services. Classes of schoolchildren are welcome to visit their local library, preferably by prior arrangement. 7 to 10 year-olds can visit the Central Children's Library for an introduction to their central library. Older pupils starting comprehensive school take part in a longer visit to the Central Library organized by the School Instruction Service, when detailed instruction in library use is given.

We can visit and talk to playgroups, Mums and Toddlers, schools and other organizations concerned with children. Please ask for further details at your local library.

There is a separate Schools Library Service at Surrey Place which lends large collections of books to all the schools in the Sheffield Education Authority. Teachers and student teachers may also use this department for personal borrowing.

Fig. 2.2

MERIDIAN CENTRE · PEACEHAVEN

PEACEHAVEN HAS A NEW LIBRARY. It is in the Community House which forms part of the new Meridian Centre, a complex of supermarket, shops and community facilities.

The new library will have a bigger and better stock than the former and the opportunity is being taken of displaying the books in a novel way. Instead of being arranged numerically by the decimal classification, books will be grouped in about 26 broad categories or topics such as The Home, Leisure, Travel, History. (A full list is given on the other side of this leaflet). In this way the books will be presented in a manner best suited to the needs of the majority of readers.

The library will also have a children's section as well as a small collection of reference books.

Within the Library area there will be an Information Service which is designed to help members of the Public in their enquiries on a very wide range of community matters such as housing, rent and citizens' rights.

OPENING HOURS *of the new library are as follows:-*

Monday	Closed
Tuesday	10.00 am — 5.00 pm
Wednesday	10.00 am — 5.00 pm
Thursday	10.00 am — 7.00 pm
Friday	10.00 am — 7.00 pm
Saturday	10.00 am — 4.30 pm

To mark this important occasion in the life of Peacehaven the County Library has commissioned a water colour from Robert Tavener, the well-known Sussex artist. This is on display in the library.

LOCATION MAP

CL.289

Fig. 2.3

Fig. 2.4

on other aspects of the services will be of any use if people simply cannot get to them when they are open. For public libraries generally, evening opening, and opening on Saturdays is normal; often for mobile libraries the stopping times are less convenient for possible users, and two or more visits per week at different times of day can be helpful. Curtailment of evening and weekend services for financial reasons can have a quite disproportionate effect on accessibility.

For school and college libraries access at lunchtimes and before and after the normal teaching day is essential. For part-time students particularly, access time is limited and an adequate service needs to be organized at times when the students want to visit. In schools, pupils are usually encouraged to use the library individually after the school day, but it is still not uncommon to find services that are available only for organized use during the timetabled part of the day. Information centres which are not housed within library service points seem to have a particular problem in arranging for services to be available outside the strict business day.

BIRMINGHAM PUBLIC
LIBRARIES

UNIVERSITY OF ASTON
LIBRARY

UNIVERSITY OF BIRMINGHAM
LIBRARY

CITY OF BIRMINGHAM
POLYTECHNIC LIBRARY

These four libraries co-operate
to provide services to readers in
Birmingham.

Catalogues. Each library has a
special union catalogue of
books and periodicals held by
the four co-operating libraries.

Referral service. Your librarian
may be able to help you locate
items or specialist information
in one of the co-operating
libraries. A letter of
introduction can be provided if
a visit is necessary.

Borrowing. Academic staff and
research students registered
with the three co-operating
academic institutions in
Birmingham can apply for
direct borrowing facilities.

Before attempting to make use
of these facilities *please ask at
your library's Enquiries Desk.*

Fig. 2.5

Environment
Throughout this book the emphasis will be on helpfulness and creation of a 'comfortable' atmosphere; surely the days have gone when silence was demanded in libraries, other than in areas set aside for study. But there are many other features that can be intimidating to users.

Heavy doors in older buildings can be a hazard to children and the elderly; polished floors can be dangerous and the sound of squeaking soles can be very conspicuous and embarrassing in a quiet building. Small changes can have a positive and surprisingly large effect: indicating if a door needs to be pushed or pulled, or explaining in a small notice that a door is out of use to avoid people with a pile of books and young children struggling pointlessly; 'please do not smoke', rather than the bald 'no smoking' could be a model for all kinds of advisory notices.

Guiding and arrangement of stock
Guiding can be a valuable part of readers' advisory work; if library users can easily find out the location of subjects in which they are interested, and can understand the way services are arranged and provided, then their use of the library will be more efficient and their opinion of the service enhanced.

Guiding begins outside the library: the premises should be clearly marked as a library or information department, in letters large enough to be easily read from the other side of the road, or down the length of a corridor. An exterior notice should also contain details of the opening hours, so that passers-by or those who arrive when the building is closed can check the library's hours. Obviously a notice such as this should be kept up-to-date, and changes in opening hours should be widely publicized and separately advertised well before they take place to avoid disgruntled patrons making wasted journeys. It may be useful to print opening arrangements on book jackets or date labels, together with information on renewals so that users borrowing books can easily find the telephone number and details of opening. Clearly it is more difficult to change such notices on every item of stock if some alteration is made; a bookmark inserted in items borrowed by each user could provide similar information and be more readily updated.

The location and style of public notices is never easy to decide; if specialized help is available it is a good idea to make use of it. In a school or college an art department may be able to help, and local authorities often have specialist display staff who could be approached. If the do-it-yourself solution is the only one possible, great care should be taken to make the result as 'professional' as possible. Scribbled, untidy notices do not effectively pass on their message, but they do pass on a different message — that the library cannot be bothered to prepare tidy notices. Hand-written notices if produced by a member of staff with a neat and legible hand can be adequate for short-term purposes (a photocopier out of order, or a jammed door) but cannot be recommended for permanent notices. Using a notice pro-forma (Figure 2.6) can greatly improve appearance.

The use of 'instant' letters of the stick-on or transfer type much improves the legibility of notices; here again it is necessary to be careful to do a neat job and regulate letter spacing and layout. Where it is possible, professionally prepared notices should be used; these are likely to be the most legible and to be eye-catching, and therefore more effective than home-made

Fig. 2.6

attempts. The house-style of the local authority or parent organization will probably be used to ensure a standard appearance. If there is no such style, it can be useful to devise the library's own simple style or logo: this clearly shows that the library has an identity and is prepared to take the trouble to develop its public face. Many library services will wish to incorporate the library symbol (Figure 2.7) into their design.

Where to locate permanent notices needs careful attention; look at the location guiding provided in supermarkets and department stores for clues. In most cases, notices should be at eye level and placed to confront users rather than at the side of corridors or entrances where they make little impact. A mobile notice-board placed just inside the entrance, and moved every few days will tend to catch the eye better than a permanent fixture. New versions of the same notice, perhaps in different colours, will make more impact than one notice left in place for several months.

The arrangement of the stock of a library can also be a help or a hindrance to readers; a simple, logical arrangement will enable patrons easily to find their way about. Broken sequences and scattered rows of shelving may be confusing. The more intrinsically 'understandable' the arrangement of stock, the more successfully it will be possible to aid readers to find what they want; detailed guiding is always important, but more so in awkwardly shaped or rambling premises.

In most libraries there are inevitable moves of stock from time to time, perhaps to accommodate expanding subjects, or to alter the appearance of the layout. This means that any system of detailed guiding must be flexible enough to allow easy alteration; guiding which takes readers to the wrong place because it has not been revised after a move is worse than useless.

Generally one or more of three basic methods of guiding will be appropriate depending on the shape and size of the premises and the type of clientele — children or college students need a

Fig. 2.7

different presentation of information, for instance. The first method is by use of a large clearly visible floor plan; the scale should be constant, sufficient information should be provided to enable a user to identify a topic, but without so much lettering on the plan that it becomes confusing to follow. If colour-guiding is employed it needs to be clearly explained on the plan. There is an obvious problem with a floor-plan that it needs to be re-drawn each time an alteration is made; in general such a plan will be unnecessary in very small, compact premises.

A second method is to provide users with a printed guide, which may incorporate a small plan. The advantage of this is that it can contain more printed information than a wall-mounted plan, users can carry it with them and consult it as they walk around, and if changes are made a new version can be printed without difficulty.

A printed guide — perhaps issued separately from the main general guide — is often the most effective way of explaining the catalogue and classification scheme in use. These tools are obviously so essential that no intelligent subject use of a library can be made without consulting them, but they are complicated to understand, and are often different in format and construction from one library to another. Where their use is always necessary, as in a school or college library, more detailed instruction can be provided, as will be discussed below, but in public branch libraries or information departments a simple, broad explanation may suffice if backed up by personal help readily available. Where there is no catalogue, or a categorization system is in use, it is necessary to provide on notices or printed guides an explanation of the categories or an index to the classification numbers in use.

The third aspect of guiding that will be useful everywhere regardless of other help provided, is detailed guiding on shelving. Every bookcase, bank of shelving, storage cabinet, magazine rack or whatever should carry a legible indication of its contents; these should appear at regular intervals, should be repeated and subdivided for long runs of materials, for fiction divided alphabetically for example, and must be capable of rapid revision when stock is moved around. Individual shelf guiding is perhaps only relevant where stock is tightly packed and new subjects cannot be marked by more noticeable means. Remember to indicate if there are separate sequences of oversize books or pamphlets.

User education

Fjallbrant and Malley (1984) comment 'one does not readily associate public libraries with user education, possibly because the educational role of the public library service is generally seen as secondary to its role as the provider of leisure-time reading and other services'. However much some might see this description as dismissive the general point is true; with a 'floating' clientele there is little scope to provide organized programmes of user education. The exception will be special arrangements made for groups of visiting schoolchildren or college students on assignments requiring material not available in their own college library, or students of the Open University or embarking on courses operated under the Open Tech scheme. For general users needing more advanced skills, a detailed leaflet explaining full use of the catalogue, or maybe a series of handouts or bookmarks outlining the abstracting services in certain ranges of topics might be appropriate.

In school libraries a programme of user education is essential: obviously it is better for the users if the librarian is a qualified person, competent to provide basic information in any subject field. Library sessions should be regularly timetabled as such, and should continue throughout the school; if they are described as part of English lessons, there is a risk that pupils will associate the library only with that subject, and the English Department will resent the loss of timetabled hours.

The basic objectives of user education will be similar in any type of library. There are four main categories of achievement:

1   That users regard the library as a place to go to find information.

2   That users recognize that library staff are a part of the information service, and should be approached for advice.

3   That users become familiar with the range of material relevant to the subjects they are studying.

4   That users can make full and effective use of the library's materials and all its back-up services.

In a school library these sessions will begin as induction courses, making pupils at ease and showing them all the range of materials. This will be followed by introduction to the catalogue, to children's encyclopedias and other appropriate materials, selected for relevance to the work the children are doing in the school. Sessions should be as attractive and relaxed as possible, putting the emphasis on practical work carried out individually or in small groups. Quizzes, crosswords or worksheets will help.

For older pupils more detailed information skills teaching can be combined with discussion groups perhaps reviewing fiction they have read, drawing up 'top ten' lists, or discussing videos, software or other materials from the library stock.

In college libraries, as in universities and polytechnics, the provision of user education should be a normal part of the curriculum, and can be more easily managed than in public or school libraries, because the subject interest and abilities of each group will be predictable. After general induction courses, which should be reinforced by a full explanatory guide, and must include information on catalogue use, subsequent sessions will be closely geared to the students' precise needs at the point of their course which they have reached. If they are provided too far in advance they will be forgotten, and obviously provision too late is unproductive; close liaison with the teaching staff is necessary to ensure co-ordination. The more successfully such courses are run, the better will be both teaching staff and student reaction to what the library can do, and the organization's general goodwill towards the library and its needs will increase.

Chapter Three

Who are your readers?

Libraries and information departments exist to serve their users; if there were no users, then there would be no purpose for libraries to exist. Retailers know very well that if they do not stock the type of goods that local people want, they will get no trade and they will have to adapt rapidly to local requirements or close down. Because libraries are 'protected' from commercial pressures, many have become lax about examining whether their stock and services are appropriate to the local people.

Years ago, it used to be assumed that libraries existed to 'improve' the public, and therefore collections of material would include good quality, highly regarded literary works, and textbooks on a range of topics.

Nowadays this approach is not valid; the nature of our society has changed in many ways: most local communities contain a proportion, maybe a majority, of people of non-British origin who will regard British classics as quite irrelevant to any aspect of their lives; for most people education is more pervasive and to a higher standard than it was a number of years ago; people generally use other sources of 'information' apart from libraries — newspapers and television obviously provide a wider general background knowledge to a range of topics and ways of life than previous generations would have known. Thus the direct need and incentive of 'self-improvement' is less apparent, if indeed it ever had much validity.

Paymasters of all sorts of library services are now more vocal in demanding to see value for money, relevance of services to the needs of those who are paying the bill. This leads to the question, what are the needs of the local community? Let us remember that the community is not just the people who use the library — because users are maybe only 20%–30% of the total population, and thus the non-users are more important and may carry more weight with local politicians, for instance — and we need to beware of vague impressions as to library use: 'hundreds of children' using a public branch library may mean only that about 20 noisy children come in each day and are very noticeable because other users are quiet and make little impact on the staff.

The process of finding out who the users and non-users are is called community profiling; in school and college libraries and information units, it can be carried out fairly simply if care is taken to do a thorough job; in public libraries it is obviously far more difficult and less reliable — but any guide is better than none at all. It is a process that every member of staff should contribute to, not only professional staff; library assistants are more likely to live in the immediate vicinity of their public library and to know a bit about local life, but their impressions need to be organized and developed into a structured profile.

When the library has a community profile, it is possible to begin planning what services to expand, and which to curtail, which categories of people never seem to use the library and what to do about it, what sort of stock should be bought to cater for readers' needs and what sort of training staff require for helping users (see Appendix 3.1 at the end of this chapter).

Public libraries

To assess the needs and wants of a local area, the question to ask first is: what is the community (Appendix 3.2)? There may be a small town with clear boundaries, but do large numbers of people come each day to work there, or shop? In city areas, what features might form a boundary — perhaps a major road that tends to prevent access, or a river with poorly sited bridges. Do people tend to visit the local shops on foot, or by bus, or by car? Having established the boundaries, who lives there? Published census returns will give details by quite small areas about age, sex, housing, employment and social class, but figures are out-of-date (1981 returns) and there is a danger of being swamped by information. Local authority housing departments, social services departments and other parts of the local government services will be able to provide basic data on age groups, ethnic origins, types of housing, levels of unemployment. Informal contact with local councillors, social workers, clergy, careers officers, business people and many other groups will help to broaden the amount of basic information on who lives in the community, what is going on in the community, and what kinds of issues currently affect life in the community. Mandy Hicken (1986) makes several useful points to aid profiling.

Analysis of other local services will also reveal details of the community structure (Appendix 3.3); numbers of children enrolled in local playgroups, the number of pupils in local primary schools, will enable us to calculate the proportion of the population under-five, and under-ten (Appendix 3.4). Similarly old people's homes and day centres will show the ratio of elderly people.

In multi-cultural areas, approach local community organizations to find out how many families of different ethnic backgrounds live in the community, and what languages they speak, and whether the need to learn English is a priority for some of them.

On the basis of the information found, the library's stock can be adjusted to achieve maximum relevance. If your area contains a large number of retired people, then plan for provision of stock that will appeal: there may be a lot of interest in gardening for example, and large-print books may be popular. Such an area may have few families with children, so extensive provision for the under-fives would be inappropriate.

Provision to multi-cultural communities will need a basic stock perhaps in several languages, and obviously staff able to read the languages and scripts at least well enough to organize the material on the shelves.

For readers' advisory work, a knowledge of the local community provides essential background on what kinds of needs are likely to emerge, therefore what sort of stock to provide. The second question to ask is: what is the purpose of users' visits to the library? The type of stock provided should reflect the requirements of users.

Public libraries have to cater for a range of potential uses: the heaviest use will probably be for recreation — fiction, biographies and popular accounts of leisure subjects for instance. If this is an important category of use, remember to cater for various levels of abilities: people pursuing hobbies and interests may need very simple introductions, or may be looking for all the in-depth material they can find. Provision of fiction must also be balanced between the needs of those seeking romances or crime stories and those who scan the reviews in the Sunday papers.

But recreation is only a part of public library use; pursuit of information on a 'hobby' can merge into a need to explore a subject area thoroughly. Such self-study may be undertaken almost unconsciously, or may be directed by attendance at courses at further education colleges, Open University courses, correspondence courses and similar facilities. The 'adult independent learner' has now been recognized as a distinct category of user that libraries should seek to help.

Other people making non-recreational use of public libraries may include children on homework assignments, business people wanting trade figures, addresses of suppliers, or commercial contacts, unemployed people seeking training or career information.

Even in the smallest service point people from all these categories and many more are likely to come in; if they are existing users, they expect to find relevant stock and expect to be able to obtain from the staff advice on what to read, or where to find information. If they are not regular users but have come in for a specific book or a piece of information, they will almost certainly be unaware what to do, or where to look and the attitude of the staff will be vital in helping them to find what they want, in which case they will come back, or in deterring them by lack of interest or basic ability, in which case potential users are probably lost for good.

Information departments

Information units cater for particular problems or for particular client groups and therefore the need to work out who is using the service may be initially less basic. However, an information department may be the most public part of an agency or commercial operation, the best place to look for details of the sort of questions being asked, and the precise nature of the clients approaching the service, and can often be asked by the parent organization to pinpoint from their activities the most pressing areas of need, or the most prominent type of client.

In a careers library for example, the range of people approaching the service and the spread of possible occupations will be limited by the provision on the one hand of various local or national Government training schemes, the qualifications that pupils and students emerge with from local schools and colleges, and on the other hand by availability of industrial or commercial opportunities. Clearly if traditional industries are declining and apprenticeships have become rare, but employment in service industries is likely to rise, then the library and its staff should become well versed in the training needed and stock appropriate materials to aid job-seekers and the careers advisers. The whole service will value comment from the library staff on the kind of demands being made, and approachable staff prepared to pass the time of day with users will often learn background information on local concerns that might not emerge from more formal interviews. This type of contact will apply in many areas of information work where the client group is known, but the exact needs from time to time may vary.

Other types of information agencies provide a certain kind of service, but never know what categories of people may approach them; for example, Small Firms Information Centres, or Tourist Information Offices hold a range of materials basic to any enquiry. But they can only efficiently respond to real user needs if they build up a profile of the typical user: what sort of firms are approaching them and with what sort of enquiries; are tourists more interested in finding out about local events, or certain major sights, or are they more concerned to find details of local accommodation. Here again it is the 'public face' of the service, the information unit staff, who must keep records of their categories of enquiry so that stocks of materials and staff training can be adapted to meet the users' needs most efficiently.

School libraries

Staff of school libraries will obviously know the basic data on their users; the numbers of teaching staff, numbers of pupils and the age range need no investigation. The needs of pupils will however differ greatly between one school and another and the library staff need to take care not to overlook certain specialized problems.

The type of area in which the school is situated will be a factor in determining the type of provision to be made. In an urban area pupils may all walk home from school and be able to visit local branch or reference libraries if they have a need to find information out of school hours. In a rural area however, pupils may have a long or tiring journey home, waiting for buses or walking long distances and they will not be able to visit other libraries in the evenings; such pupils might well prefer to remain at school after the end of the timetabled day to begin homework projects provided that school transport arrangements do not preclude this.

For any area, the availability of other library services will affect what the school library does; where there is a nearby public library with good stocks the school library can put its emphasis on the school's requirements, but where there is no other accessible service the school library may try to provide a general lending-library service of fiction and non-fiction appropriate to the age range. For such a purpose it will be necessary to discover the leisure interests of pupils so that relevant stock can be built up.

In multi-cultural areas the school library obviously has a vital role to play in backing up the teaching staff; the stock of the library and the methods of access can be developed in the ways most helpful to particular children's needs.

Clearly, the reading ability of all pupils must be assessed; if there is a high proportion of pupils with reading difficulties or low reading age, it is essential to provide a balanced stock that such pupils will find attractive and manageable, while not neglecting the needs of more able children.

The academic work of the school must be familiar to the library's staff: to ensure co-ordination of the library's provision with current teaching, staff should take pains to become aware of what is scheduled to be taught, and to which groups of pupils, and by what methods. Learning activities that place the emphasis on the pupils' initiative to find information for themselves are very satisfying for the school library, but all the staff need to be aware of what is going on, and to be prepared to give relevant help without embarrassing interrogations to find out what the pupils are trying to do.

For pupils at a more advanced level, the syllabus of new public examinations will provide the library staff with the basic data on which to plan stock purchases. It will also be necessary here for the staff to liaise closely with teaching colleagues so that they are aware of the materials available and can make best use of the library's limited budget.

Outside the academic curriculum, the needs of pupils to find out about training opportunities, further education, and careers, can be handled by the library: as with other services, knowing the community can help the library staff plan provision, and enable them to become prepared to advise users effectively.

College libraries
The community of a college library may include a number of
special categories of students whose needs must be itemized so
that provision can be weighted towards groups with the greatest
problems.

A community profile would begin by listing the various
courses taught in the college and noting the numbers of students
on each course, and in each year of the course. The range of
subjects and the depth to which they are studied need to be
considered as factors in buying a balanced stock. Co-ordination
of the library's activities with the methods of the teaching staff
will obviously be essential.

The nature of the students will affect the structure of the
service; many colleges are finding their intakes comprise greater
numbers of 'mature' students — an umbrella term taken to
mean anyone over the traditional student age group. Such
students commonly have other commitments and whilst able to
attend the college during the timetabled sessions may have very
limited time to spend in the library outside those hours. Similarly
part-time students will be very restricted in their 'spare' time
while at the college, and may need to take home materials that
their full-time colleagues need to have available all the time.
When the profile reveals how many such students there are as a
proportion of the whole enrolment, the library will be able to
judge how big a 'problem' they have and adapt its systems to suit.
For example it may be necessary to introduce a separate
collection of key texts for the use only of part-time students, or to
adapt the rules of a reserve collection to make borrowing easier
for part-time students.

Numbers of disabled students, or students from various ethnic
backgrounds who will have special difficulties should also be
noted. A properly constructed profile will enable the library to
decide where to place its priorities, and to resist undue pressure
to over-resource particular courses because of staff demands.

Categories of students likely to have difficulties will benefit
from the construction of a profile as all library staff will become
aware of their existence, will be able to plan how to meet their
difficulties, and the students should find a sympathetic and
knowledgeable response from any member of staff whom they
approach. Readers' advisory work is not just a matter of
providing information but also of helping readers to obtain and
use relevant materials, and planning the service to make this

possible for all students will help to achieve this need. Mature students and part-time students will also be those with the least knowledge of the library; their lack of time and unfamiliarity with the college will place them at a disadvantage, so particular help during induction courses and having suitable staff available to assist them when needed — which may be at 'inconvenient' moments like lunchtime or at five o'clock — should be a planned part of their provision.

Students attending short courses, for a day or week, will also of course be unfamiliar with the library; their likely needs should be written into the profile, along with staff needs for teaching, development and research, and any special features that need to be catered for, such as links with local industry.

Assembling a community profile is therefore valuable in any type of context; readers' advisory work depends on knowing likely demands from patrons and being equipped to meet them. This can only be realistically achieved by careful prediction, and this should be an essential preliminary to any organized attempt at advisory work.

Note. Appendices 3.1 to 3.4 are taken from *An analysis of the community served by Southwick Library.* This forms volume two of the Borough of Sunderland's package *Profiling the community: a practical guide for librarians.*

Appendix 3.1   A community profile
Southwick Library is a well-established library with a wide-spread catchment area. A decline in book issues in recent years may be due to reduced opening hours and a lower level of expenditure on new stock.

The population of the area is expected to remain fairly stable, with the predominantly youthful age structure gradually becoming more balanced in composition. There is limited space for new housing within the area, therefore the library can expect no sudden increase in demand.

The level of affluence of the area is low, and the majority of the population are "blue collar" workers, traditionally not the most regular users of the library's services. However, library membership is only just below the national average.

The biggest factor influencing the future use of the library is the high level of unemployment which, in spite of plans for the revitalisation of local industry, is unlikely to decrease to any significant extent in the near future. Thus the library can be assured of a large number of potential library users.

A high proportion of the population are children, with just over a third of this number being members of the library. Distance from the library is one factor preventing a higher junior membership. Visits from local schools have been successful in encouraging children to use the library, but it is just as essential to encourage the parents to allow their children to join the library. Modernisation of the interior of the library and many holiday activities for local children are some of the means which have been employed in order to counteract the slightly forbidding appearance of the outside of the library.

There is also a high proportion of young people in the area, many of whom are unemployed. Publicity in local youth centres and meeting places may increase interest in the library. Many of those who do not visit the library ask about the Central Library's video lending service, so perhaps in future this service may be extended to Branch Libraries.

There are fewer old people in the area than in Sunderland generally, but they are still a potentially high user group. Library provision for those unable to visit the library because of age or disability is fairly well established. It may be possible to increase such provision in the future if there is sufficient bookstock.

Southwick then, is an area with high levels of unemployment and social problems, with many people living solely on state benefits. It is also an area with a strong community spirit, and with the help of the Community Librarians Team, the library can play a vital role in the integration of information and advice agencies in the area.

[Borough of Sunderland: Department of Recreation and Libraries, 1985]

Appendix 3.2   Introducing the catchment area
The catchment area for Southwick Library lies north of the River Wear and can be divided into several areas. Southwick itself is an old village, now largely re-developed, which expanded dramatically with the prosperity of the shipyards and glassworks at the turn of the century, before being incorporated into Sunderland Borough in 1929. However, this prosperity has

declined to such an extent that in 1979 Southwick was designated an area of need.

To the north of Southwick lie the housing estates of Carley Hill and Witherwack, with Red House and Downhill housing estates in the western half of the catchment area.

To the south lies the River Wear, and the industrial areas of Low Southwick and North Hylton Road.

Southwick Green serves as the main district shopping centre for the housing estates in the area.

There are several plans affecting the area:

1   The North Area District Plan, which covers the whole urban area north of the river and west of the Sunderland-Newcastle railway line.

2   The Southwick Green Action Area Local Plan, which forms part of the North Area Plan. Several traffic control and environmental improvement schemes have already been carried out.

[Borough of Sunderland: Department of Recreation and Libraries, 1985]

Appendix 3.3   Analysis of local services

Health
Community health services are based at the health centre in Southwick Green. However, people living in Downhill may use Hylton Castle health centre, which is situated just outside the catchment area.

The services available at Southwick health centre include: ante-natal sessions, child and school health, dental, chiropody, family planning, cervical cytology, speech therapy, ophthalmology, audiology and pharmacy. There are also 6 G.P. consulting suites.

In addition there are two chemists, four dentists and one optician practising in the area.

Sunderland Disablement Advisory Centre, in Southwick Road, is open to all disabled residents of Sunderland who need advice on all aspects of disabled living.

There are also Women's Health Groups, particularly the 'Change of Life Support Group' run by Carley Hill Tenants and Welfare Rights Centre. Women's health sessions are held regularly in Southwick health centre.

There is no hospital provision in the area, the nearest hospitals being Monkwearmouth, and the General Hospital across the river.

Implications for the library
The library is on the other side of a main road to the health centre in Southwick. However, the library is on a popular bus route, so many patients will pass the library on their way to the health centre.

Posters to publicise the resources of the library, particularly the stock of leaflets held in the Community Information Collection, could be displayed in the health centre. This collection includes a large number of books and leaflets on health and disabilities, which are heavily used.

The Community Librarians Team, based in Southwick Library, ran 'Books from Birth' sessions at Southwick health centre for four weeks to publicise the library and its resources.

The library's noticeboards are used to display posters from various groups dealing with health problems.

[Borough of Sunderland: Department of Recreation and Libraries, 1985]

Appendix 3.4 Analysis of local services

Education
The catchment area contains a wide range of schools, from nursery schools to secondary schools.

Nursery Schools   St. Columba's Nursery   60 places
                     Hylton Red House Nursery   39 places

Primary Schools	Age Range	Expected Roll	Admission Number
Bishop Harland C.E. Primary	3–11	193	30
Nursery Class			26
Carley Hill Primary	3–11	223	45
Nursery Class			26
Downhill Primary	4–11	135	30
English Martyrs R.C. Primary	4–11	217	45
Hylton Red House Primary	4–11	358	60

Southwick Primary	3−11	441	70
Nursery Class			30
St. Hilda's R.C. Primary	3−11	140	27
Nursery Class			26
Witherwack Primary	4−11	150	45
Secondary Schools			
Hylton Red House School	11−18	1370	300
St. Thomas Aquinas R.C. School	11−16	578	150

Maplewood School is a special school dealing with children aged between 8 and 12, and Emsworth House is an assessment centre for young people.

Just outside the catchment area is the Monkwearmouth College of Further Education, which will become a tertiary college in 1986. Many of the students pass Southwick Library on their way home, and several classes have visited the library for research purposes.

Southwick Centre, a community college, is housed in the former High Southwick School, which is a few hundred yards away from the library.

Because of falling rolls, proposals have been made to close St. Thomas Aquinas School in September 1986 or 1987, the pupils being divided between St. Robert of Newminster in Washington, and St. Anthony's school south of the river. Hylton Red House Secondary School will also be affected, as proposals are being made to remove the sixth form.

St. Hilda's R.C. Primary and Southwick Primary Schools are both regular users of the library, classes coming to the library whenever possible. Other schools find the distance from the library too great a barrier to regular use of the library.

There are five playgroups in the area. The Southwick mother and toddler group is supplied with books by the Community Librarians Team.

Implications for the library
As schools find their bookfunds drastically cut, so more use is made of the library's resources. Teachers are therefore encouraged to bring classes to the library, particularly as, because of parental indifference or the distance from home, these visits may be the only chance these children will have to use the library.

The schools' own resources are supplemented by the books and project collections provided by the Schools Library Service.

Southwick Library has a total junior bookstock of 6,934 volumes — 4,034 fiction and 2,900 non-fiction. The non-fiction stock is heavily used by children for projects, and therefore when choosing bookstock it is necessary to consider the subjects being taught in the local schools.

The junior books in Southwick Library have been arranged in broad subject categories on the shelves. This arrangement is similar to that in several local schools and has proved popular with the children. In view of the heavy use made of the junior non-fiction stock, it is essential that replacement stock is bought quickly and regularly. Shelf capacity in the junior library is 5,750, and a further 1,000 books could be accommodated.

[Borough of Sunderland: Department of Recreation and Libraries, 1985]

Chapter Four

Answering readers' questions

This chapter is concerned with the questions that patrons may ask in libraries, and the methods of dealing with them; in the following chapter we shall look at the kind of questions that may be asked outside the traditional library context – mainly community information that is handled by public libraries and specialist information units.

For the present therefore, we are considering readers' questions in libraries; the audience for this book was defined in the Introduction as staff in smaller libraries, public, school or college, without immediate access to information resources apart from the stock on their own shelves. So, this chapter will be simply based; it will discuss how staff should approach the answering of questions, what types of questions can be identified, and how to answer basic enquiries.

Grogan (1979) and others have noticed that people who want help prefer to find their own way to it if they can; this is why it is so important to provide ample guiding and written help for users. If people cannot find what they want, many give up easily, or having wasted a lot of their time eventually and grudgingly sense defeat and ask questions in a negative manner – 'I don't suppose you've got anything about fish.' The first step any library employee can take to avoid these situations is to ensure that the environment of the library looks helpful and welcoming, that there is clear basic guiding, that there are plenty of invitations to ask the staff for help; but the main feature that will make a success of answering questions is having staff who look as though they might be helpful, and who are accessible.

Few people will approach staff who look unwelcoming; if your natural expression is a frown and your manner brusque you will attract few enquiries – a positive, helpful attitude is essential. Similarly, staff should be accessible to answer questions: if all off-the-counter jobs are done in a back room then the only person available to help users may be already too busy with lending procedures at the counter.

Thus, we need a policy, regardless of the library's size: do we have a separate desk where a staff-member sits expecting questions, or do we hope that enquirers will ask whoever is on duty at the counter; in a single-person library, how will you deal with a question if you have other users waiting and the telephone ringing?

It is reasonable in any small library to expect that all staff will have received training in the use of a small range of basic reference sources, will know how to handle a simple enquiry, and will know how to deal with something which is obviously too complex for the library to handle. We shall look later in this chapter at how to handle enquiries, and suggest a small range of basic sources; for enquiries that are too big to tackle or require specialist materials, a procedure is necessary to route the enquirer to a more appropriate source. In a public library system, there should be a procedure guide so that staff can react quickly and efficiently (for example, see Appendix 4.1). This will avoid wasting enquirers' time and patience, and will indicate that questions are expected and that there is a system of tackling them.

In independent libraries, a small school library for instance, there should still be an agreed procedure for referring enquirers elsewhere if it is a question beyond the library's own resources. Referral is not an admission of defeat: it is unreasonable for a small organization to carry a large reference stock or to train its staff to cope with complex problems that may arise only seldom. A re-direction to a larger, specialist library will help users more quickly and avoid staff time spent in searching for information unlikely to be found. Staff therefore need to know what material is available in their own library, and to be familiar with other local resources: if a school librarian needs to refer senior pupils to a local reference library it is inadequate merely to tell them to go there. The library should be contacted and an arrangement made to expect the pupils at a certain time and the nature of their enquiry indicated. Many staff in small libraries will find it very useful to visit other local services regularly so that they become known to the staff there, and find out what sort of reference materials are available. There is a world of difference from the user's point of view in being told to 'try the reference library', and being advised after a phone call that 'Miss Smith in the reference library says she will be able to help you; please ask for her or for Mr Jones. The library stays open until 8 o'clock.' You need only take a little trouble to make a big impact.

How to handle questions
It is very important to take enquiries seriously; however trivial the question might seem, it is sufficiently weighty from the user's point of view to merit visiting the library to ask. If we accept that the greatest part of public library use is for recreational purposes, then it is not logically possible to deny assistance to readers attempting quizzes and crossword puzzles, although of course regular enquirers can be 'trained' to look for themselves in a limited range of likely sources.

A reader has the right to have a question treated attentively and an attempt made to deal with it. Many simple enquiries are locational − the answer is a direction to that part of the library where the appropriate material is kept. Clearly such an enquiry can be dealt with competently by any member of the library staff. Some library authorities (Figure 4.1) make a formal arrangement to train staff in locational enquiries by using a questionnaire which encourages them to think about what their own library has in stock, and what other resources there are within the whole library service. There is still scope to check availability with the appropriate department or other service point, and not to send a user to the central library to look at PRESTEL if the system is out of order this week. Even within the small branch library, it is more courteous and helpful to take the reader to the relevant place rather than merely point to the part of the shelves where you remember seeing what is wanted.

Not only is it courteous, it may well be that readers will chat to you as you walk them to the place where they need to be, and in doing so tell you what they really want. Finding this out is the first essential step in dealing with an enquiry, and is called the 'reference interview'. Appendix 4.2 shows the type of problems that can arise: questions can be vague, terms like 'China' (Figure 4.2) can be ambiguous.

The purpose of the interview is to make sure that you really understand the question that is being asked, and that you know the sort of answer that is required; an enquiry about South African exports might require an answer that records simple facts − fruit, gold, coal − or it may demand actual figures for the volume of exports, or it may be that the enquirer wants to know what effect economic sanctions would have. These questions would each be answered from different sources, so it is necessary to find out what is really wanted at the outset.

It is helpful to find out all possible background information

| INFORMATION SKILLS CHECKLIST | | |
CAN YOU USE?	DO YOU HAVE IMMEDIATE ACCESS TO?	WHERE DO YOU REFER PEOPLE TO?
NEWSPAPERS		
INDEXES		
BIBLIOGRAPHIES		
ENCYCLOPAEDIAS		
DICTIONARIES		
ATLASES		
STREET PLANS		
TIMETABLES		
PRESTEL		
CAREERS INFORMATION		
COMPANY & PRODUCT INFORMATION		
TOURIST INFORMATION		
EDUCATIONAL INFORMATION		
STANDARDS & PATENTS		
ON LINE		
FINANCIAL INFORMATION		
STATISTICAL INFORMATION		
TELEPHONE DIRECTORIES		
STREET & TRADE DIRECTORIES		
PROFESSIONAL DIRECTORIES		
BASIC INFORMATION KITS		
ELECTORAL REGISTER		

Fig. 4.1   Training questionnaire (City of Bradford Libraries).

A request for a book on China could mean:

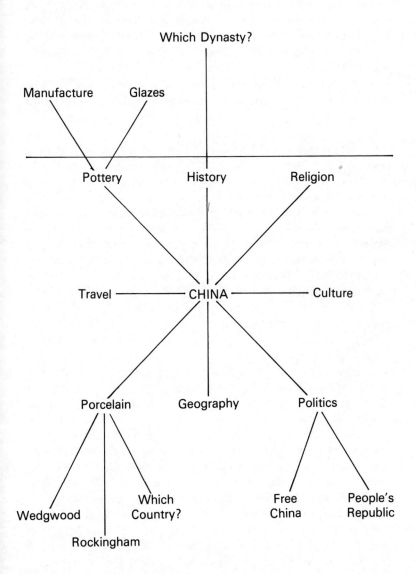

(Leicestershire Libraries and Information Service)

Fig. 4.2

that might provide clues on where to find the answers; make sure the enquirer has not misunderstood a vital fact − something heard on the radio, or read in a book perhaps − and is thus not altogether clear what the real question is; beware also of false impressions, conclusions automatically reached that might be mistaken − the South Africa enquirer above might have wanted figures for an essay on Southern Africa in the 1930s.

The level of information required needs also to be determined; many questions can be answered in general terms from an encyclopedia, and perhaps two short paragraphs of information maybe five years out-of-date will be quite adequate for some purposes, but it will not suffice for a local firm seeking commercial information. Chatting to the enquirer as you walk to the shelves can enable you very informally to get to know what you need to answer the question.

Cross-check facts if you can − population figures for example may differ widely between various sources − and locating a second book will show that your concern is not just to put anything in front of the reader and go away. If the question cannot be easily answered on the spot because the library is very busy, or you feel it will take too long to do it there and then, or if the enquiry has been received by telephone and it is unreasonable to make the enquirer wait several minutes, then an accurate record should be made of what the question is, who the enquirer is, where he or she can be contacted. A pro-forma may be used to ensure you collect all the essential data, but the key points are to tell the reader what is going on, and to ensure that the request gets put into whatever system the library has for dealing with enquiries.

Nothing is worse than the enquirer hearing nothing further from the library; if the answer cannot be found the reader must be contacted as soon as possible and advised of the problem. Other sources might be suggested if appropriate, but it is unhelpful to refer people to other libraries unless you have checked to find out if they are likely to be able to help.

All staff should get to know what the enquiry procedure is, so that they can advise the reader of who will look at the question and how long it might take; the reader might prefer to contact the central library in person if the enquiry is urgent rather than wait for a branch to pass on the details. Readers cannot expect miracles from their library, but they are entitled to prompt and helpful attention.

Types of questions
Enquiries directed to libraries can be divided into two basic
types: questions concerned with books and other library
materials (bibliographical questions) and questions concerned
with facts or subjects (reference questions). This second category
will include questions on community information, and this area
will be fully discussed in chapter 5.

The two basic categories can be further subdivided, and the
eight divisions listed by Grogan (1979) seem to represent an
agreed consensus that covers all possible enquiries:

1   Firstly there are simple directional or administrative
questions:
− What time do you close today?
− Where are the atlases?
Obviously there is a simple answer to these questions; any
member of staff should be sufficiently aware of the library's
layout and routines to be able to deal with them, and good
guiding will make most such enquiries unnecessary.

2   Straightforward questions relating to the library's stock
form the second category. These questions will ask for a
particular book, recording, videotape etc.:
− Do you have that cookery book by Rabbi Blue?
− Do you have a copy of *A town like Alice?*
These questions will be answerable from the library's catalogue,
or if there is no catalogue, from a central bibliographical unit
that can be contacted by telephone; checking of further details
can be done from simple bibliographies that we shall discuss in
the next section of this chapter. It will be faster and more
successful before we search further for staff to check the title of
the cookery book, and the author of the novel. After training it
would be expected that all library staff would be competent to
use the catalogue and simple bibliographical sources: however it
appears often to be overlooked.

3   The third group comprises simple questions of fact:
− What's the population of Birmingham?
− Which is the longest river in the world?
Such questions should be answerable by all staff even in the
smallest libraries; a satisfactory answer demands familiarity
with only a small number of reference works and we shall
propose an appropriate range of titles in the final section of this
chapter. Remember to use more than one source if possible to
cross-check the answer; even simple 'facts' often turn out to be

variable depending on the source, and the reader should be made aware of this to avoid the library being criticized for supplying 'wrong' information.

4   The fourth group consists of subject enquiries (material-finding questions):
− I want to find out how to make wine.
− What's the history of the Statue of Liberty?
These questions are not limited to a simple, factual answer; they are 'open-ended' enquiries where the amount of information available depends on the resources of the library and the needs of the reader. Thus there is no 'correct' answer, and the reference interview approach discussed earlier needs to be used to find out what the enquirer actually wants to find out, and how much information is expected. This is obviously more complicated for inexperienced staff to tackle; basic reference sources and the library's catalogue can supply an answer that might be adequate, and this could be handled by any member of staff. If fuller or more specialist information is needed, the procedure agreed for tackling more advanced enquiries should be put into practice − to consult a senior member of staff if there is one available, telephone the central library, refer the reader elsewhere, or whatever system the library operates as its policy.

The remaining four groups of enquiries are probably beyond the resources of a small library and would definitely need specialist assistance:

5   'Mutable enquiries' are those which seem simple but turn out to be problematical − requests for books that cannot be traced; historical information that is in dispute, for instance.

6   Research-type enquiries where no answers can reasonably be found from the published literature, but a full-scale investigation is needed to determine the 'answer'.

7   Miscellaneous enquiries which often contain some flaw − proof of the flat earth theory perhaps.

8   Unanswerable questions: these are either for information that no-one has ever bothered to collect, or possibly for information that is deliberately suppressed. Occasionally it is possible to find printed confirmation that a 'fact' is unknown.

We have seen that this full survey of all the types of enquiry conforms to the two basic categories introduced at first: bibliographical enquiries and reference enquiries, and we shall now consider how to approach each of these categories.

The basic work is well within the abilities of all library staff-members, and a simple training programme, regularly repeated, will enable most simple enquiries to be quite adequately dealt with by even the smallest library.

Few questions are 'unacceptable' in libraries; generally they will be enquiries that demand too much clerical effort to be feasible ('I need the titles of 50 books about modern warfare') and the solution is to advise the reader to come and scrutinize the catalogue or bibliographies personally. Aside from this, everything can be either tackled or referred — the library's policy on how to do this should be clearly understood by all the staff.

Bibliographical questions

Many readers' questions relate to the stock of the library, or to problems over the availability of particular books or other library materials. The provision of sources to answer these questions is very wide, and in this chapter we shall concentrate only on the major, basic resources. 'Bibliography' is strictly concerned only with books and other printed materials, but the term is used here to cover any materials stocked by the library; this will probably include recordings, videotapes, or computer software.

Enquiries will relate firstly to particular items — books by a certain author, a periodical with a known title, a recording by a particular performer. These author/title enquiries may be simple to answer if the library possesses a copy of the item, or users may be seeking to discover whether such an item exists. The library's own catalogue is the first source to consult; it is always useful before starting to make sure that the reader has accurate information on the item in question. If the author's name has been spelt incorrectly it may not be possible to find it in the catalogue; if the title of a book is only remembered by the reader, it might be vague — 'a glossary of computer terms' might be found to be *Computing terms: a dictionary,* for example. If possible ask the reader where the information came from; if from a newspaper review further details might be mentioned that the reader has not given, such as the publisher's name. Knowledge of how to use the library's catalogue should be a priority for all staff, and many libraries have devised simple exercises to train people in their use (Appendices 4.3 and 4.4), not confined of course to the bookstock catalogue (Appendix 4.5). The catalogue is a complicated tool, assembled at great expense, and it is absurd not to use it fully. It will need careful explanation if readers are to make use of it correctly, and before this can take place we need to be sure that staff can handle it competently.

Where the library has no catalogue there should be a known procedure to cope with author/title enquiries; this may be a phone call to a central union catalogue, or only taking details for a later request. Although most independent school or college libraries will have their own catalogue, some small public library service points may not; increasingly microfiche catalogues (COM-fiche) are coming into use, and a master copy of the whole system's holdings can be available at all service points. Where this is not so, staff should be trained in what the library expects them to do to make good the omission.

To check readers' information for accuracy, to find books by title, or to find out the titles of books available by a particular author, the basic source is *British books in print*;* this is now available in microfiche and contains details of all currently available British books arranged by authors' names, and by titles. It is regularly updated. (A printed version is also available, but is unwieldy and becomes out-of-date; on-line and CD-ROM versions are becoming available, but the microfiche is likely to remain the most common format for the immediate future.) Staff should all be familiar with *BBIP :* it is easy to use and provides ready access to the most commonly sought information.

Some libraries will take other services that perform related functions — the *Bookseller,* a trade paper recording new publications, or the *British National Bibliography (BNB)* assembled by the British Library. Much English language publishing takes place in North America, and some libraries will also have copies of American equivalents — *Books in print* (also on microfiche) or the *Cumulative book index* (CBI).

Where such basic materials are held by a library, it is inexcusable not to train all staff in their existence and coverage, and encourage them to use them when readers ask author/title questions.

These titles all deal with *current* materials — items in print and available at the present time. If readers ask for older material, books that seem to be out-of-print, the library

---

*From October 1987 to be known as *Whitaker's books in print*, and available on CD-ROM.

catalogue may help, but if not, bibliographies covering earlier years need to be checked: such retrospective bibliography is probably beyond the scope of a basic training scheme.

The second area of bibliographical questions relates to subject information — books about given topics, where an item is not specified, but any book on the subject might be appropriate.

For subject enquiries, the library's catalogue is the major source; if there is no catalogue, staff should have access to, and be fully trained in the use of an index to the classification scheme in use, or the coverage of categories in a categorized stock. A fiche catalogue recording the stock of other libraries in the system may be very helpful here, but explain to the reader that items cannot be immediately available. When appropriate topics have been located in the catalogue it is important to take the reader to the shelves to look at what is available at the time. If the material does not seem to be what is required, try to find out why; perhaps the level is wrong — too detailed when only a simple introduction is needed or vice-versa; perhaps the stock is out-of-date, perhaps material with more illustrations would be helpful.

Advise the reader from a further check in the catalogue about other books in stock that may not be on the shelves at present; perhaps there is a title *A beginner's guide* . . .; information on publication date, numbers of illustrations etc. should be on the catalogue entry and will assist in selecting a suitable item.

It is then necessary to explain what steps can be taken to enable the reader to gain access to the required item; perhaps a central library or district library may have it on the shelves — a phone call will find this out. The reader may be happy to reserve the item, but point out that a fee is often payable for this service and there will be a delay; if the reader is particularly interested in a book located via a bibliography that is not available from the library system, perhaps an inter-library loan would be appropriate — this decision will be in the hands of the senior librarian or specialist staff, and advice will need to be sought.

Always keep the reader informed of what is happening, and explain that some processes involve a time delay; sometimes a reader will prefer immediate information even if not quite satisfactory rather than have to wait.

Subject enquiries that cannot be answered from the library's own catalogue will involve investigation in a large range of published sources; in some contexts it might be appropriate to train staff in the use of one or two such items if the library covers a special subject field, but generally their use must be considered to be outside our introductory scope.

Fiction is a particularly interesting area, and in public libraries is a very important part of the stock. The great majority of fiction enquiries can be answered from an excellent series of volumes published by the Association of Assistant Librarians:

Fiction index (annual, and five-year cumulations)

Junior fiction index (5th ed., 1985)

These titles arrange newly published fiction under a series of broad subject headings so that readers can obtain ideas of further authors to try if they like particular themes.

Sequels : adult books (8th ed., 1986)

Sequels : junior books (7th ed., 1982)

These two volumes list fiction written in a sequence featuring the same characters, the same family, or the same geographical location.

Simple practical exercises can be devised to ensure that staff can offer assistance in fiction (Appendix 4.6) — a frequently neglected part of enquiry activity.

The very small number of simple sources quoted in this section cannot be comprehensive, but if all staff were aware of them, and how to use them, the great majority of all general bibliographical enquiries could be readily and helpfully answered.

For audio-visual materials and the enquiries that may arise about them, staff should become familiar with the 'Gramophone' series of guides to recordings, and such titles as the *Penguin video source book* and the *Video source book U.K.* for checking information about videotapes. Regular scanning of relevant magazines will be the most successful means of keeping up-to-date with new productions.

Questions relating to magazines — titles, subject coverage, frequency or cost — can be answered at a general level from the annual publication *Willing's press guide,* which includes information on newspapers and all popular periodicals.

Reference questions

Requests for factual information form the other major area of enquiry work. There is no limit to the number of reference books that a library might purchase, but except in very large libraries provision will consist of a limited range of volumes — sheer cost will prevent further additions and the use made by the library's patrons will determine how far this part of the collection needs to be developed.

Here as in bibliographical questions it is very important to find out what level of information is needed: whilst some questions will be very straightforward − 'Who is the local member of Parliament?' − many more will seem vague, and an adequate answer will be impossible unless the precise enquiry is first established. It needs also to be remembered that some questions have no single, watertight answer; for example it is not possible to find out how many books are published in the world each year, and current population figures for Egypt vary depending on the source consulted.

The whole stock of the library can be used to answer questions; because an item is not in the reference section, it must not be excluded as a source of information. A good quality, recent textbook or general non-fiction account of a subject may give all the information that an enquirer needs, and if it can be borrowed it will be an advantage.

The simplest policy for stock provision to be used for reference purposes is to concentrate on stocking a small number of titles, and providing effective staff training so that all staff know how to use the material. Ten reference volumes that all staff have been trained to use will provide a more satisfactory small-scale enquiry service than 50 books that only one or two staff have examined.

The cost of reference materials is so prohibitively high that generally only a very small collection can be maintained; it is very important to keep the sources up-to-date − a five-year old reference title is probably useless for most purposes.

Reference books should be selected for their authority − well-known publishers and established titles, reviewed favourably − secondly for their accuracy and objectivity, thirdly for their currency − are they up-to-date and are they re-issued annually? − and fourthly for their arrangement and presentation − it must be possible to find information without delay (Appendix 4.7).

Staff should be trained to use all the material readily: this will involve examining the contents pages, indexing method and general structure of the work. Most libraries will find it simple enough to devise exercises that illustrate the features that should be noted (Appendices 4.8 and 4.9). Harrison and Beenham

(1985, pp.132-70) also suggest the type of material to look at, and provide a sample assignment.

A small quick-reference collection would need to include a selection from the materials listed here, supplemented by works that relate to the library's clientele — the *Education year book* (Longmans, annual) in a school library for example, or the *Stock exchange official year book* (Macmillan, annual) if simple questions on companies are often asked.

- Encyclopedias: a good general encyclopedia is essential, *Britannica* if possible, or *Everyman,* supported by a simpler single-volume work such as *Pear's Cyclopedia.*
- Dictionaries: the *Shorter Oxford English dictionary* might be appropriate, or a smaller source such as *Chambers dictionary.* A general dictionary of abbreviations such as *Everyman's* will also be useful.
- Factual sources:
    Whitakers almanack (Whitaker, annual)
    Britain 198 — (HMSO, annual)
    Municipal yearbook (Municipal Publications, annual)
    Statesman's yearbook (Macmillan, annual)
    Kelly's business directory (Kelly's Directories, annual)
    Annual abstract of statistics (HMSO, annual)

This might form an adequate range for general purposes. It is vital to provide good staff training, particularly with a volume such as *Whitaker's almanack* which contains such a quantity of material. All these items should be replaced each year to retain their currency; some libraries may replace every two years to save costs, but any longer delay than two years makes the material very unreliable.

- Telephone directories: all the local phone books for the area, and Yellow Pages.
- Timetables: local bus schedules, British Rail timetables, and possibly services from a local airport. Currency is obviously essential.
- Geographical sources — a good quality atlas and gazetteer, perhaps the *Times atlas* or an equivalent. Street maps for local towns, Ordnance Survey maps for the region, local guide books and hotel lists.
- Literary sources:
    Oxford dictionary of quotations (OUP) or an equivalent
    Roget's thesaurus (various editions available)

> *Brewer's dictionary of phrase and fable* (Cassell)
> *Freeman's Everyman's dictionary of fictional characters*
>   (Dent)

- Biographical sources:
    Who's who (A. & C. Black, annual)
    Dictionary of national biography − DNB (OUP) might be
    affordable in some contexts.
- Miscellaneous: a teletext receiver can provide a great deal of
  information, and in a format that patrons will find
  attractive. PRESTEL is a very valuable information source
  and should be seriously considered by many more small
  libraries.

Training can be simply organized for all these sources, so that
staff can go to the most likely source and know how to locate
information in it. Readers should only be left to browse for
themselves in reference materials if they clearly wish to do so;
many patrons will find it impossible to cope with an unfamiliar
arrangement.

If the reader cannot wait for an answer, or if you are dealing
with a telephone enquiry, take all the relevant details of the
questions, and the name and contact information of the
enquirer and deal with the question with the minimum of delay.

For difficult questions, or enquiries clearly beyond the scope
of your library, as has been stressed before, an agreed procedure
must be in operation for passing the enquiry on to a more
appropriate source; the reader should also be kept informed of
progress, and should feel that the question is receiving serious,
competent and reliable attention.

If staff are trained to answer simple questions, know the
procedure for referrals, and are courteous in handling
questions, then all readers can feel satisfied that they are getting
a fair service within the limits of the library's resources.

Appendix 4.1 Enquiry technique training − notes for teams

1 Brief explanations of attitudes to Library Assistants.

2 *Recommended procedure on receiving enquiries*

   At District Libraries
   1 If a team member available, direct enquirer to this
      person.

2   If no team member or this person engaged make *one* attempt to find information.

3   If information cannot be found ring Ashton Reference Library, or ask team member to undertake enquiry if now available. Put enquirer on phone.

At Categories 2, 3, 4 Libraries

1   If team member present direct enquirer to this person.

2   If not, have a quick look in Reference Collection for information.

3   If information cannot be found ring District Library or if engaged Ashton Reference Library.

N.B. Get all details and *confirm enquiry*

3   *Telephone Enquiries*

At District Libraries

1   If a team member on duty pass the enquiry on to this person.

2   If no team member on duty, ask enquirer if they wish to hold or for Library Assistant to ring back.

3   If they hold take details of enquiry and look in *one* place for information. If it cannot be found tell enquirer that you will ring back — ensure that all details are taken (i.e. name, telephone no. extension etc.) Then ring Ashton Reference Library.

4   If enquirer does not wish to hold initially then take all relevant details, and follow same procedure as in 3 above.

At Categories 2, 3, 4 Libraries

1   Follow same pattern as for District Libraries, except that District Library should be contacted first before ringing Ashton Library for help.

[Tameside Libraries and Arts]

Appendix 4.2 Role-plays
These can illustrate situations where things can go wrong in
enquiry technique.

Face to Face Enquiry

Enquirer	Do you keep population figures?
Assistant	Just a minute, I'll find out. *(Dashes off to ask team member in office)*
Assistant	Do we keep population figures?
Team member	Where for?
Assistant	I don't know, I'll find out *(To enquirer)* Which population figures do you want?
Enquirer	Oh, round here.
Assistant	*(To team member)* He says, round here
Team member	Where is round here? Ashton, Waterloo, Tameside, GMC., Istanbul?
Assistant	Oh, I didn't ask, I'll find out *(to enquirer)* Could you be more specific, is it Ashton you want or somewhere else?
Enquirer	Well, really, it's Mossley population figures I want.

(End Of Sketch)

Question to Library Assistants — What went wrong in the
sketch?

[Tameside Libraries and Arts]

Appendix 4.3 Exercise on use of the catalogue
1 Put the following lists into the order in which they would
   appear in the catalogue:

Death Valley	New, Samuel P
Deadwater	New York
Dead Sea	Newark

De Soto	New, S. Patricia
De Grey	New Scotland Yard
Dee	Newlyn
D'Anvers County	New, S.P.
Deer Lake	Newbridge-on-Wye
Deal	Newcastle
Debica	New, Charles
De'Ath, Edward James	New London
De Bono, Edward	Newcastleton

Using the catalogues find:

2 The name of a book by:

  a) Gillian Naylor   b) George Rudé
  c) Iris Murdoch   d) Paul Klee

3 What books the library has by:

  a) Thomas Hardy   b) Gunther Grass

4 If the library has books with the following titles:

  a) Bring On the Empty Horses
  b) Loser Takes All
  c) Foreign Mud
  d) Captain Swing

5 Where on the shelves you would find books on:

  a) Portuguese art   b) Thermodynamics
  c) World War I   d) Scottish Law

6 List what the library has on the following:

  a) Tony Benn   b) Gang-warfare in Glasgow

7 Using the available bibliographies find:

  a) a book on canoeing published in the 1970s
  b) a book on Thomas Mann
  c) a book by Edward De Bono
  d) who publishes *Cider With Rosie* in hardback
  e) what editions are in print of *Women in Love*

f) how much is the paperback edition of *Ulysses* by James Joyce

g) what is the ISBN code for Gower Publishing

h) what is the ISBN for Kafka's *Metamorphosis* in paperback

8 Imagine you are ordering the following items. Write down all necessary details:

a) A book about cats by T.S. Eliot

b) Any book about Vikings

9 You are asked by a reader for information about the writer H G Wells. Using the catalogues, bibliographies and any other sources, draw up a booklist of about 10 items. Do not forget to cite author, title, publisher and date for each one, and if it is in the library add the classmark.

[Sheffield City Polytechnic]

Appendix 4.4 Practical exercises using the microfiche catalogue

1 Author/title sequence

(a) Is there a book by M. de Pace entitled *Working with dBase II: The Personal Computer Database* in the catalogue? What is its Dewey number, and in which libraries is it located?

(b) How frequently is the *Directory of Publishing* published? Which libraries keep it, what are their holdings, and where is it shelved?

(c) How many titles do we have issued by the Manpower Services Commissions Office for Scotland?

(d) What is the title of no.86 in the 'Hobart Paper' series? Who wrote it? Which organisation publishes the series?

(e) Which libraries have the British Council's annual report? In which library would I find the reports published between 1955 and 1960?

2 Subject sequence

(a) Find a book on coal industries in South Africa.

(b) Find some directories of schools in Great Britain.

(c)   Find books on computer aided design in the United States.
(d)   Find a book on codes of practice in the motorcycle industries in Great Britain.
(e)   I am interested in books on shopping hours in Great Britain. What headings would I need to look under to be sure of seeing all the relevant entries?

3 Bibliographies – Questions
1.   Who publishes the *Secret Diary of Adrian Mole Age 13¾*?
2.   Write down the full bibliographic details of Huw Beynon's book *Working for Ford*.
3.   How often is the *Kent News* published?
4.   When was *Library* established?
5.   Where would you find statistical information on ferry services?
6.   How much would it cost to take out a subscription to *Kim*?

[Department of Trade and Industry Headquarters Library. Exercises from a training course for clerical officers and new professional staff.]

Appendix 4.5
Answer the following questions using the COM Record Catalogue:

1   Which District has a copy of Mendelssohn's Preludes and Fugues for Piano, Op.35 played by A D'Arco?
2   Is there a recording of 'Cymbeline'? Please give details.
3   What category of recorded sound is 'Nonsuch for the Dulcimer', by Roger Nicholson?
4   Who wrote the music for 'The Desert Song'?
5   Which district has a copy of '25 years at the Aldeburgh Festival' a Decca boxed set. What is the SBN?
6   Have you got anything by the military band at Sandhurst?
7   What is the SBN for a record of Christmas music recorded by St. Paul's Cathedral Choir?
8   Are there any complete recordings of Offenbach's 'La Grand Duchesse de Gerolstein'?
9   Have you a recording about the Great Exhibition of 1851?
10   The P.I.L.L. French language course devised by Brian Dutton – is it found on record or cassette? How many parts are there?

11   Will I find Paul Simon's music under light vocal, pop or folk
     in the browser box?
12   I know you have a humorous record by someone whose
     name begins with a B. Could you give me a few helpful
     suggestions?
13   I would like a recording about garden or woodland birds.
     What alternatives can you offer? I have already heard a
     cassette about wild birds.
14   Who were the soloists in Britten's own recording of his
     Spring Symphony?
15   Have you any Japanese Koto music?
16   Can you find any jazz recordings by Ted Heath which are in
     stock?
17   Who reads the diary of Samuel Pepys? Is it on a record or
     cassette?
18   Have you a poetry reading of 'The Story of Ossian'?

[Nottingham Public Libraries]

Appendix 4.6   Practical exercise (fiction)

1   Reader requests *The West Pier* by Graham Greene. Find
    details.
2   What's the name of the new Catherine Cookson?
3   Who wrote *The Burning Shore?*
4   Who wrote about a Japanese policeman called Otani?
5   Who wrote the books of the following films?
        Avalanche Express
        The Rape
        Candleshoe
        Ryan's Daughter
6   What is the latest book by James Michener?
7   Is there a sequel to *Treasure Island?*
8   Which Hornblower novel follows chronologically after
    Hornblower and the Hotspur?
9   Suggest some authors who write stories about sailing ships.

[Staffordshire County Library]

Appendix 4.7

Reference sources for quick factual information
Any item in a library provides information; if a person wants information about the Yorkshire Dales, it may mean that she's going on holiday there and wants to know something about the life and history of the area, in which case a guide book or travel narrative to take away and browse would be required, or she may want to know the exact area of the Dales National Park, or the population of Wensleydale, or the dates of major agricultural shows. For the second category of question libraries usually assemble a small collection of printed sources that provide answers to quick, factual questions.

There are maybe hundreds of possible items that could be used; listed on the attached sheet are a basic selection of general reference works. Most quick reference collections in public libraries would contain these items, and probably several others that staff experience had found to be useful.

Getting to know a reference source
There are just 2 main points to consider in evaluating reference sources — content and arrangement.

CONTENT would include the following —
    is the coverage comprehensive?
    is the material up-to-date?
    is it accurate, authoritative, reliable?
    is it balanced, or biased?
    what level of information does it contain?

ARRANGEMENT would include —
    how easy is it to access the information?
    are there contents pages, indexes, headings,
    cross-references?
    are tables, dates etc., clearly laid out?
    is the book easy to handle?
    is it made to stand repeated use?
    does it give clues to other sources?

[Leeds Polytechnic School of Library and Information Studies]

Appendix 4.8

Reference sources

"Quick reference" enquiries.
The actual answer is not important, but please note *where* you
found it (which book, which page) and *how* you found it (using
index, or contents page etc.). Make a note also of any difficulties
you found in using the sources.

1 Has Alastair Burnett ever been editor of the Daily Express?
2 What does "cop-out" mean?
3 How big is the British National Debt?
4 What times are the Sunday morning trains from Leeds to
   Appleby?
5 What's the name and address of the Bishop of Wakefield?
6 What are the Harleian mss (manuscripts)?
7 In which book does Oliver Mellors appear?
8 Find a brief statement on how British film censorship
   works.
9 Who was British open golf champion in 1974?
10 Find a list of firms in the Leeds area (or your local area)
   making up-and-over garage doors.

[Leeds Polytechnic School of Library and Information Studies]

Appendix 4.9

Basic reference skills

Using the available reference books, answer the following
queries. List all the sources you tried.
1 Who is the MP for Bolsover?
2 What is the local paper for Whitby?
3 What is the address of St Martins School of Art?
4 What is the telephone number of the Tate Gallery?
5 What is the address of the Post Office Philatelic Bureau?
6 Who is the chairman of British Rail?
7 Name a plumber in Chesterfield.
8 Are there any corset manufacturers in Leamington Spa?
9 What products are manufactured by Hodge, Clemco Ltd
   of Sheffield?

10   Is there an association for sufferers of asthma? What is the
     address?
11   When did Gladstone first become Prime Minister?
12   Who was the first man killed by a railway train? When?
     Where?
13   What is the symbol for aluminium?
14   What element is number 24?
15   What are the dimensions of A3 size paper?
16   What is the population of Tanzania?
17   In what county is Dunwich?
18   What does James Callaghan list as his interests?
19   What is the address of the publisher Thames & Hudson?
20   Where is the nearest DHSS office?

[Sheffield City Polytechnic]

Chapter Five

Community information

The previous chapter dealt with general information requests which can be answered from books and other published items. To this aspect of readers' advisory work another area of activity has been added — community information.

Community information relates to a particular area, neighbourhood, or group of people, and includes all types of local information; public libraries have become very involved in this work because they are located in local communities, have trained staff, and premises which are open at times when people are able to make use of the service. But in addition, a great many other agencies have set up information centres to deal with particular types of information or particular areas of need.

Some of these agencies may be run by local authorities, or national bodies, and some by volunteers and charities. Some of them offer advice rather than information. This is a distinction which libraries must be careful about; if you advise a patron to take a particular course of action, then you can be held responsible if something goes wrong. Generally libraries and information units exist to help their users by explaining solutions to problems and directing enquiries to relevant bodies, and do not attempt to offer counselling services — these are the business of qualified workers.

The growth of information agencies demonstrates the need that is not met by existing sources; people living in an urban area finding they have various problems might turn to a number of possible enquiry points, for example:

Public Library
Citizens' Advice Bureau
Consumer Protection Agency

Community Education Council
Careers Office
Job Centre
Community Relations Council
Town Hall Information Service
Community Health Council
Sports Council
Council of Voluntary Service
Social Services Department
Housing Information Centre
Chamber of Commerce
Development Corporation
Money-help Centre
Post Office
Tourist Information Office
Small Firms Information Centre
Local Newspaper
Local Radio Phone-in
Literacy Scheme
Ethnic Integration Advice Service
PRESTEL and local Gateways

This list could never be comprehensive; more agencies come into being to meet new needs — the spectrum of what is 'information' and the number of people handling it grows and grows. The staff of these information centres or information units are as much involved in 'readers' advisory work' as are their colleagues in public libraries, school or college libraries, or information centres in commercial firms or industrial companies: they are the intermediaries between the users on one hand, and a mass of written, printed, recorded information on the other.

Although the subject areas will differ, the aspects of the job are the same as those discussed in previous chapters: to get to know the users' needs, to get to know the information stored in the library or information centre, and to match up the required piece of information to the question a user has asked. The techniques of readers' advisory work still apply.

What is community information?
Community information generally does not consist of tidy, published books; it is information contained in Acts of Parliament, Statutory Instruments, regulations of the DHSS,

local legislation and bye-laws, the 'small-print' of financial agreements and guarantee forms and similar bureaucratic documents; or it may be information on local clubs, societies, agencies, schools, further education classes and child-minders — all these types of information relate directly to people and their day-to-day problems. It is 'soft' information, which means it is difficult to pin down, variable according to the status of the person asking the question, and variable from one area of the country to another, between one local authority and another, between one town and the next. Because it relates directly to people's immediate needs, questioners cannot wait too long for an answer, and they certainly cannot be given a reference book to browse through.

The reason so many agencies have appeared is that so much highly specialized and rapidly changing information is now produced that it is very difficult for a general service, such as a public library, to make a detailed collection of more than a small part of it. Specialized agencies have more success in their own small field, but have a fragmented approach.

The organization that is approached first of all by an enquirer needs to be efficient in establishing the patron's needs (the 'reference interview' process), to be familiar with its own sources, and to be skilled at referring enquiries on to appropriate local authority departments or other agencies for further assistance.

How to collect information
If staff are to be able to use the community information collection effectively, they should all be involved in assembling it. This should ensure that staff become knowledgeable and aware of local interests, activities and events, and so are better able to discuss points with patrons and provide appropriate answers to questions.

One good way of starting is to walk around the local area and observe what is about you; some clear social points, on age and type of housing for instance, will be noticeable. Observe the location of schools, old people's homes, doctors' surgeries, playgroups etc. Notices in shop windows, church hall notice-boards, post offices, and community centres will give you a clue to the type of activities that are held locally; look at local newspapers, free and priced, to see announcements of local societies' meetings.

It will also be useful to keep in touch with local developments by reading local council minutes and planning applications.

If you attend some local meetings you will become better informed on what local societies are doing, and you will be able to meet people who are taking an active part; these are the contacts that you need to develop in order to ensure that you receive, and continue to receive, news of future activities and meetings. Other contacts will be informal; talk to the staff in day-care centres, doctors' surgeries, dentists' waiting-rooms, to find out if they would display notices about your service, and make them aware of the service you can offer, so that they can refer to you people who mention problems that might be handled from the information collection.

Most of the material that is collected will be your own notes, and pamphlets or information sheets from local groups and societies. It is helpful to your patrons to maintain this local collection of material in an up-to-date manner; a collection will become rapidly out-of-date and the information centre will need repeatedly to renew its contacts and obtain fresh material.

It is a useful training strategy to insist that new staff walk around the area noting points that strike them, and checking how their findings compare with your files. Are there new clubs in the area whose notices you haven't seen before, or new group secretaries, new hours of opening at the local council offices? Asking new staff to make a check for new material either by telephone or by using a standard letter will help them to get to know what range of material is covered by the collection, and the key people involved.

Where the information centre is run by only one person, or where no new staff are employed, it must be regarded as essential continually to revise the material held; if the collection is not current, then you risk wasting your own time and your patrons' time in pursuing out-of-date contacts or acting on old information.

Regular, scheduled meetings with other community workers can help to identify unknown problems, and provide a co-ordinated approach to particular client groups. Such meetings might include local clergy, local councillors, youth leaders, a social services representative, community leaders if there are ethnic groupings, a representative from the Job Centre, a member of staff from a local college, and other people who personally or by virtue of their association with a local organization can help in knowing what is going on in a community, and what can be done to help.

Mandy Hicken and Ruth Kaye (1986) quote documents from Derbyshire Library Service (Appendix 5.1) which summarize the points made here. A second item from the same source (Appendix 5.2) emphasizes the need for this type of information gathering; readers' advisory work depends on your knowledge of your own material. If you have a regular hand in collecting the items in the collection, you are much better placed to help users, because you will be familiar with the type of problems they may have, and will have an idea of which groups, or which files of information might assist.

Use of community information

In the following chapter we shall discuss the physical organization of materials collected. The immediate uses of the collection of community information cover four activities: firstly, the provision of a local community information collection allows local people to have access to files of information to help them with day-to-day problems, and local concerns and interests. Awareness of the existence of such a collection makes community groups more aware of the value of publicity, and most will write some basic information for inclusion. Users such as local councillors will have a valuable summary of local activities, and the information centre may develop into a base for local contacts — a central role in the community. Secondly, staff will be enabled to carry out readers'/users' advisory work more successfully because they will be aware of local interests and activities, and better able to relate to the local clientele. As we have previously seen, knowledge of the background to problems and the type of context in which the questioners find themselves will help staff understand the need for the information, and the type of response that will be appropriate.

Thirdly, this awareness of community needs and the recording of the types of questions asked will be a vital contribution to the policy of development of the parent organization; if the information centre is based in a public library, then the development of the library's stock both of reference materials and general lending items can be geared to the interests of local users as revealed by the examination of the local area. This will be a continuous process, allowing the library to adapt to new demands and putting itself in an ideal position to predict these demands as new needs arise, rather than respond to them at a later stage when the immediate urgency is past. Clearly readers' advisory work is more efficient where the stock of the service is relevant to likely requests. Where the information centre is run within another type of organization, a housing information centre perhaps, or independently, like the CABx, the information gathered and the problems brought to the centre's notice will help the organization as a whole to develop its work in response to precise local needs.

Fourthly, the establishment and operation of a community information service will have a positive role in information transfer in the locality: an informal network may emerge whereby various bodies will use the service as a central point for publicity, or will run help-sessions at the information centre as a means of getting their existence known, or will invite staff to participate in activities to get a fuller knowledge of the work that the various bodies are doing. The simplest device may be a community noticeboard where all local groups prefer to display their publicity: this may be 'adopted' by local newspapers or local radio as their collection point for information, and the information centre may itself organize a regular typed listing of events for distribution to other focal points in the community.

The collection of community information will therefore be of great importance in helping staff to develop their 'feel' for readers' advisory work and will place the library or information unit in the forefront of community life. This will increase its use and lead to other benefits in the development of an overall service.

Appendix 5.1
The library itself holds information about a section of the community i.e. library users. An analysis of the membership files will supply information about their age (in broad categories), sex and place of residence and this may usefully be compared with those of the community as a whole.

An examination of a random sample of between 10 and 15 per cent of a library's membership cards would give a very accurate picture of the library's users. (The sample is made random by choosing the starting point at random i.e. if a 10 per cent sample is being used choose a number between 1 and 10 out of a hat, start there and follow with every tenth card).

A major source of information about any community is the

people who live and work in it. An important step in constructing a profile is to question them. This can be done formally or informally:

(a) Informally — this is the method which will be used most often and involves simply talking to people either face to face or on the telephone in an unstructured way.

(b) Formally — using social survey techniques, e.g. questionnaires and structured interviews; a method which will not generally be used except in special circumstances because of the expertise and resources required.

Examples of the types of people to be questioned include doctors, councillors, health visitors, social workers, clergy, teachers, careers officers, youth workers, playgroup organisers, businessmen, trade union officers. Contact can also be made with ordinary residents in pubs, shops, at public meetings and, of course, in the library.

N.B. Take care not to raise expectations, which you will be unable to satisfy, in terms of enhanced library provision to specific groups. Explain that you are merely engaged in an exercise which will improve the library's ability to respond to needs throughout the community.

The final step in profiling is the process of observation. A very accurate impression of a community can be gained by any librarian who simply cares to look about her/himself. Examples of the kinds of points to look for are as follows:

(a) Housing — is it council, private, owner-occupied, in multi-occupation, of what standard, is it specialist, e.g. Housing Association, Housing Co-operative, Sheltered Accommodation?

(b) Shops — are there large supermarkets with car parks or small corner shops, any shops selling goods for ethnic minority groups, are there many selling secondhand goods, what end of the market are the consumer durbales aimed at?

(c) Recreation — are there sports halls, squash courts, football/rugby pitches, golf courses, social clubs for the elderly or young, bingo halls, theatres, cinemas. What does the nature of provision suggest about the age and social class of the community?

(d) People in the streets — how do they look, how are they dressed, are they all of English origin?

(e) Look at graffiti (or absence of it!)

[Derbyshire Library Service]

Appendix 5.2
Recording/storage of information
Information will need to be structured as it is collected –
probably by collecting it under preconceived headings. Within
each heading or subject area the information should be stored in
such a way that it is easily retrievable. A variety of methods may
be employed to ensure this, for example, information about
local societies, schools, churches, etc. is easily handled on cards,
while statistics relating to population distribution are probably
best represented in map form. (The type of information which
could be collected within certain subject areas is illustrated
below.)

Remember that the process of profiling, particularly in
making contact with people in the community, is as important as
the end product, i.e. the files of information.

Associated uses of the community profile
Beyond merely building up the knowledge of library staff about
their community and its needs, there are other important uses
for the information gathered.

1   It can form the basis of the library's community information
    service.
2   It is of considerable use in stock building, as it can point to
    the materials needs of different groups within the
    community. Additional investigative and statistical
    procedures can be devised to provide a highly accurate stock
    profile of the community but in the initial stages of
    community profiling it is recommended that consideration
    of this possibility should be deferred.
3   Through the contact made with individuals and groups
    during the course of profiling, knowledge is obtained which
    will enable publicity about library services and activities to
    be directed in an appropriate manner at specific points in
    the community.

N.B. A community profile is never finished. Communities are
in a constant state of change which means that the building of
the profile is a continuous process.

[Derbyshire Library Service]

Chapter Six

Keeping Track

Chapters 4 and 5 dealt with answering readers' questions, either from the bookstock, or from the community information collection. To develop your skill in readers' advisory work and check that your collection of materials is adequate, it is useful to keep a record of the questions you are asked, and note where the answer was found.

Keeping records of your activities is a normal part of library or information unit routine; it is valuable even in a one-person unit to remind you of your decisions on certain types of materials or procedures, and will help your successor understand what was done, how, and why. Where there is more than one member of staff, a procedure manual will ensure that everybody does the same thing with regard to any aspect of the service, and does not make an individual ad-hoc decision that may be unknown to other staff, or changed by action at a later date.

In a larger organization like a public library service it is clearly necessary to ensure that all parts of the service share the same policies and procedures, and a centrally prepared staff manual will be provided. Sylvia Webb (1983, pp.30-1) gives a brief but comprehensive list of points that should be covered in a procedure manual.

Whether or not there is such a manual in your service point, it is a sound idea to supplement it by collecting query information. We have noted previously that if a query cannot be adequately answered on the spot, then details must be taken for subsequent action or referral. To ensure that staff remember to make an acceptable summary of the question and have established with the enquirer how quickly the answer is needed, what level of information is required, any background points that may be useful, and how to contact the reader later, it is useful to have a pro-forma enquiry record that will cover all these points. It also has the effect of showing the reader that a procedure is being followed and is likely to be successful.

A possible simple record sheet is shown in Figure 6.1. Bunch (1984, p.71) shows an alternative idea. Whether the answer is found in your own service point or whether the enquiry needs to be passed elsewhere, a copy of the enquiry record should be retained; this can be consulted if the reader subsequently asks about progress, but the main purpose of keeping the record sheets will be to enable a picture to be built up of the types of questions received and the success found in answering them.

Over a period, by checking back through the records, it will be possible to find trends that will help you to plan your stock provision and staff training; if you receive many questions about gardening topics, it will be a good policy to expand your stock in this area. It may be justifiable to purchase an encyclopedia of gardening if you can prove from your records that it will be frequently consulted and could have answered two enquiries per week last year that had instead to remain unanswered or referred elsewhere. It may of course be possible to balance the cost of this against the saving on not replacing another reference item that has never served to answer any questions at all — if you keep a record you will know which item this is.

Bibliographical and reference enquiries

For items that are answered from the bookstock, or should be answerable from it, your enquiry records as they cumulate will show the subject range, the frequency with which questions are asked, and the time it takes to answer them — both the staff time consumed, and the delay before the reader actually gets what is wanted. The figures will demonstrate how time-consuming readers' advisory work can be, and are a powerful argument both in favour of efficient staff training, so that the minimum time is wasted in initial confusion and searching inappropriate sources, and in favour of a well-understood referral system so that problem queries can be sent on to specialists without delay.

Records will also enable you to evaluate the service you give; it may be that readers wait five days for answers to bibliographical questions because requests are transmitted by written notes to a central unit, dealt with there, and returned also by note. If local staff have access to *British books in print*, *Fiction index* and *Sequels*, perhaps with training 50% of questions could be

ENQUIRY   RECORD

                                        Date:
                                        Service Point:
                                        Assistant's name:

Reader's name:
Address:
Telephone number:

    (note   best time of day to contact:

ENQUIRY:

BACKGROUND:

WHEN NEEDED:

LEVEL OF INFORMATION:

For office use only
LOCAL SOURCES CHECKED   (e.g. Britannica, British Books in Print)
COMMENTS OF BRANCH SUPERVISOR:
REFERRED TO REFERENCE LIBRARY (date and contact)

Fig. 6.1

answered in five minutes? This may seem optimistic, but if records are kept it will be possible to find out such basic statistical information on your service, and build up a case for developing and improving unsatisfactory performance.

Records should also show where answers were eventually found, whether from your own stock or reported if from elsewhere: when similar enquiries are received in future, it will save time if staff can refer to work done previously. Obviously staff cannot leaf through heaps of old records, so it is necessary to index the record forms by type of enquiry − 'history', 'science' perhaps will suffice − and after material has accumulated for a few months it should be re-organized into a more readily findable format. Possibly information could be transferred onto a master record illustrating types of enquiry rather than specific examples; this process will enable the library or unit to build up its own training package, all the more relevant because it consists of the library's own questions. Staff can thus grow familiar with a summary of questions asked in their own service point, and how they were answered; this can be referred to easily when further enquiries are received.

Community information enquiries

We saw in the previous chapters that community information usually has to be collected by the information unit or library itself, also that the information is either 'soft' − unpublished material assembled on local clubs and societies − or 'hard' − pamphlets, benefit rates, VAT regulations etc. − and both categories need to be organized by the service to make them accessible and keep them up-to-date.

For 'soft' local information, the service must decide how the material is to be collected: a simple form should be devised to ensure that the necessary data are obtained and appear in a regular format. In a small community, the minimum information will be:

● name of the organization
● secretary's name, address and telephone number
● function of the organization
● membership details
● dates and places of meetings.

It is better to confine efforts to providing essential information only, in a form that can be maintained, rather than to be over-ambitious and assemble a large quantity of material that cannot be kept current. Bunch (1984, pp.72-3) lists a fuller basic series of points to check in assembling local society information.

Storing this information and keeping it accessible will depend on the amount of material available from the community and the resources the service possesses; a simple method is preferable if the quantity of material is small. This could be just a typed list, or a box of cards, or a strip index. A typed list can be photocopied, but cannot be easily updated; a strip index can hold only a limited amount of information and the strips can be troublesome to insert; a card index cannot be easily copied and is not very portable. A microcomputer with a very simple information handling program, or only a word processing capability, will be very useful here, if there is one available in the service point.

A home-produced file, whatever its format, could also include details of local statutory and semi-official organizations and details of local medical and dental services.

As the quantity of information grows, it will be necessary for efficient readers' advisory work to divide the material by subject to make finding particular items easier. Such subject headings should be as simple and straightforward as possible, and use normal language terms — 'doctors' not 'medical practitioners' for example.

The service might make itself better known by circulating a list of this information: perhaps a pamphlet of four pages carefully typed and photocopied and distributed to ten or so community centres, day centres, doctors' waiting rooms, newsagents' windows and similar public locations will advertise the existence of the collection, bring in more material, and attract a better standard of information from the organizations mentioned. A monthly list of local meetings can be similarly prepared, using the local press, notices, and information provided as a basis. This kind of list helps to avoid clashes of dates and makes the collection more of a real centre of community activity.

As the collection gets larger, and particularly if it is to include 'hard' information — pamphlets and regulations — a more sophisticated system of organization will be needed. Appendix 6.1 shows an example from Derbyshire Library Service illustrating the division of a large collection into a series of subject headings, with a note of sub-headings used, and an important 'scope note' feature, which guides staff to the relevant

section both when filing information and when finding it for
users. Such a system is very successful, but it has to be fully
understood by all staff, as users will require assistance to find
what they are looking for. The most efficient form of initial staff
training may be to have a regular session maintaining the
collection: this will be a time-consuming business. The
collection will need daily tidying, and replenishment. Keep one
copy of every leaflet as a master for re-ordering purposes. Out-
of-date information must be removed and replaced; if every
item is date-stamped on receipt it will be easy to check how old it
is. Material which has been well-thumbed and looks shabby
should be replaced.

A regular programme of maintenance will encourage staff to
become familiar with the contents of the collection, and make
their readers' advisory activity more successful. Staff should also
be encouraged to suggest additions to the collection from their
own reading or leisure activities; newspapers and popular
magazines often offer advice and information, perhaps in
response to readers' letters, and the articles or replies can
summarize advisory agencies and services in a convenient way. A
photocopy of such appropriate material could be included in the
collection, and organizations named should be approached for
fuller details.

Regardless of the size and contents of the collection, regular
updating needs to be an essential activity. Organizations,
societies, local DHSS offices and all other sources need to be
contacted annually at least by letter and asked to provide
current information. It is important to follow up these requests;
if no reply is received it is not adequate to forget about it until
next year. A telephone contact or personal visit to the
organization's office or secretary may be necessary; as
mentioned above, it is better to offer a limited range of material
in good condition and up-to-date, rather than an ambitious
collection that is beyond your resources to maintain.

Some further services may arise from the compilation and
maintenance of a community information collection. In some
organizations, a school or college maybe, it will be useful to offer
a personal current awareness service to interested members of
staff; a careers specialist may appreciate scanning all new
material on careers before it is filed in the collection. This will
ensure its fuller use, and will encourage staff and library to liaise
and co-ordinate their activity.

In an information unit, the key member of the parent organization may need to be kept informed on new developments: seeing new material as it is received by the unit, or receiving a regular report summarizing activities and newly collected material should help to achieve this.

If it is possible to use a microcomputer in the organization of material, a number of additional services may be possible: we have already mentioned simple updating and printing out of information on local societies, and lists of meetings. Microcomputers can also offer training facilities for staff and regular users of a collection. A step-by-step program illustrating important points in using the material may appeal to certain categories of users — schoolchildren using careers information for example.

Microcomputers can also be linked to other local services, and a local network of information services may result; this may be very informal co-operation or may be formalized, such as sharing a database to provide a fuller service — a link from a public branch library to a Job Centre possibly.

It is important that collections of information that are in use for readers' advisory work should be well maintained, kept up-to-date, and that staff are fully trained in their use. Otherwise an expensive resource is being created which cannot justify its costs because it contains old information, or cannot be exploited by staff who are unaware of its potential.

Appendix 6.1 System for organizing community information

PROBLEMS?
COMMUNITY INFORMATION CAN HELP TO SOLVE YOUR EVERYDAY PROBLEMS

Community Information is a collection of leaflets and booklets about jobs, housing, money matters, your rights, family matters etc.

To find the information you need, simply look up the subject in this alphabetical list and you see the main headings under which that information is filed in the collection.

e.g. BENEFITS   see <u>MONEY MATTERS</u>
      JOB SHARING see <u>EMPLOYMENT</u>

If a subject you are looking for is not listed, try to think of another word instead:

e.g. Accommodation – Housing

A list of main headings and what they cover can be found in the coloured pages at the end of this guide.

If you have any difficulty, please ask the staff.

We can also tell you about other organisations which can help you e.g. Marriage Guidance Council.

Please note:

1. Illnesses are not in this alphabetical list. They are filed under <u>HEALTH</u>

e.g. Asthma   is found under <u>HEALTH</u>
      Rheumatism   is found under <u>HEALTH</u>

2. Charities and voluntary organisations are not in this alphabetical list. They are filed under the subject they are concerned with:

e.g. NSPCC   is found under <u>CHILD WELFARE</u>
      Age Concern   is found under <u>ELDERLY</u>

3. Abbreviations are not listed. Look for the complete spelling:

e.g. VAT   is found under VALUE ADDED TAX.

4. All welfare benefits information is filed under <u>MONEY MATTERS</u>: Benefits.

MAIN HEADINGS WITH APPROPRIATE SUB-HEADINGS AND SCOPE NOTES

MAIN HEADINGS	SUB-HEADINGS	SCOPE NOTES
1. ANIMALS (636)		Animal welfare organisations, birds, horses and horse riding, pets, quarantine, rabies, safety, vivisection, wildlife.
2. BUSINESS INFORMATION (650)		Accounting, bankruptcy, co-operatives, exporting, importing, insolvency, small businesses, Value Added Tax.

MAIN HEADINGS	SUB-HEADINGS	SCOPE NOTES
3. CHILD WELFARE (649)	Child Health Nurseries and Playgroups	Accidents, adventure playgrounds, babies, bed wetting, bottle/ breast feeding, child minding, child abuse, diet, gifted children, pre-school children, safety *NOT* disabled children.
4. CIVIL & EQUAL RIGHTS (323)	Race Relations Sex Discrimin- ation	Anti-racism, arrest, civil liberties, data protection, equal opportunities, gay rights, harassment, human rights, immigration, minority groups, police, prisons.
5. COMMUNICA- TIONS (001)		All television stations, cable television, Ceefax/Oracle etc, computers, Information Technology, media, newspapers, Post Office, publicity, radio, telephone, video.

MAIN HEADINGS	SUB-HEADINGS	SCOPE NOTES
6. CONSUMER ADVICE (343)		British Standards, complaints, consumer protection, credit, faulty goods, food additives, furniture safety, mail orders, Office of Fair Trading, Trading Standards *NOT* Electricity, Gas, etc.
7. DEFENCE (355)		Arms race, disarmament, nuclear weapons, peace movement, radiation.
8. DISABLED (362.4)	Aids Access and Mobility Education and Training Mental handicap Recreation	Blind, deaf, disabled children, guide dogs, partial sight, sign language, talking books *NOT* Mental Health, special disabling diseases, eg, Muscular Dystrophy.
9. EDUCATION (370)		Adult education, Adult Literacy, City and Guilds, corporal punishment, Open University, schools, student grants, suspension

MAIN HEADINGS	SUB-HEADINGS	SCOPE NOTES
		NOT pre-school education, sex education.
10. ELDERLY (362.6)		Day care, general health and welfare, hypothermia, retirement, safety *NOT* fuel costs, pensions.
11. EMPLOYMENT (331)	Health and Safety at Work Training Schemes Unemployment	Dismissal, early retirement, Health and Safety at Work, industrial diseases/injuries industrial tribunals, Job Centres, job sharing, Manpower Services Commission, maternity leave, rights at work, redundancy, self-employment, Trade Unions, unemployment, working abroad, Youth Training Schemes.
12. ENERGY (644)		All types of fuel, disconnections, fuel bills, nuclear power.

MAIN HEADINGS	SUB-HEADINGS	SCOPE NOTES
13. ENVIRONMENT (711)	Countryside Planning Pollution	Bridle paths, common land, compulsory purchase, conservation, countryside, ecology, footpaths, forestry, land reclamation, lead, litter, National Trust, nuisance, public enquiries *NOT* Animal wild life.
14. FAMILY (306.8)	Death Family Planning	Abduction, adoption, battered women, care orders, cohabitation, divorce, fostering, genetic counselling, marriage, one-parent families, sex education, sterilisation/ vasectomy, widows/ widowers, wills/probate.
15. GOVERNMENT (350)		Census, Common Market, councils, elections, foreign aid, local government, Parliament.

MAIN HEADINGS	SUB-HEADINGS	SCOPE NOTES
16. HEALTH (610)	Addictions Alternative Medicine Heart Disease Mental Health Women's Health	All illnesses, Community Health Council, dental care, diet, eye care, fluoride, health treatment abroad, immunisation, mental health, National Health Service, nervous breakdown, nutrition, phobias, pregnancy, sexually transmitted diseases, suicide.
17. HOUSE & HOME (363.5)	Safety & Security	Builders, building societies, compulsory purchase, condensation/ damp etc, council housing, estate agents, eviction, grants, home improvements, home safety, housing repairs, landlords, mobile homes, rates, rent, security, squatting, tenants.

MAIN HEADINGS	SUB-HEADINGS	SCOPE NOTES
18. INFORMATION & ADVICE SERVICES (360)		Citizens Advice Bureau, Samaritans, telephone advice services *NOT* specific subjects, eg. British Pregnancy Advice Service.
19. LAW (340)	Legal Aid	Courts, crime prevention, criminal injuries, guns, jury service, Justice of the Peace, lotteries, Police, prisons, rape, shoplifting, vandalism.
20. LEISURE (790)		Activities, Duke of Edinburgh Award, farm trails, National Parks, playgrounds, sport, youth clubs.
21. MONEY MATTERS (332)	Benefits	Benefits, Income Tax, insurance, Pay as you Earn, pensions, student grants, taxes.

	SUB-	
MAIN HEADINGS	HEADINGS	SCOPE NOTES

22. TRANSPORT &
TRAVEL
(380)

Boats, canals, cars, fares, fuel consumption, Green Cross Code, lorries, public transport, road safety, seat belts, theft, travel concessions *NOT* lead in petrol, community transport.

23. VOLUNTARY
GROUPS &
ORGANISATIONS
(361)

Charities, city farms, committees, community newspapers/shops /transport, fund raising, good neighbour schemes, meetings, self help groups.

[Derbyshire Library Service]

Chapter Seven

Publicity and promotion

As was discussed in the Introduction, use of a library will be more pleasant for patrons if the atmosphere is welcoming and helpful. Hepworth (1951) stressed the value of customer goodwill, and compared the behaviour of a 'good tradesman' anxious to ensure that customers did not go elsewhere. Users of libraries may have little choice of anywhere else to go, but their frequency and intensity of use will be coloured by the attitudes of the staff.

This chapter will consider three components that make up publicity and promotion: firstly the general level of public relations that makes the service known and encourages use, secondly standard items of publicity such as annual reports and library guides, and thirdly specific areas of publicity activity — booklists on particular topics, displays, or storytimes for example.

Public relations
'Public relations begin with that first welcome smile from the assistant at the counter and runs through the efficient charging and discharging of materials, the general appearance of the place, the help offered, the stock and the services available. In fact, everything that makes up a modern library contributes to our good public image.' (Harrison and Beenham, 1985, p.192.)

Readers' advisory work we have seen depends very much on patrons being aware of the library's existence, and their confidence that their enquiries can be adequately handled. Both these considerations will be helped by sound publicity. There is a need to tell people what libraries can offer, as the majority of users are unaware of the full range of services that are available and non-users have no knowledge whatever of what the library is doing.

Public relations are important in any library, in the ways that our quotation suggests, but also outside the library in getting the service known. Ours is an 'advertisement-led society' (Sherman, 1971) and presumably advertisers find there is a response to their work.

Direct advertising methods such as posters or leaflets were suggested in chapter 2, and these need to be supported by the involvement of library staff in community activities. In a school library staff might become involved in a library club, or take part in other activities − a computer club perhaps − where the library has a role to play. In colleges, the provision of induction courses needs to be repeated in formal or informal ways as students begin new topics or new projects. In the public library, staff can join local societies and clubs and take opportunities to mention how the library can support their activities. Traditional methods of local involvement, such as talks to Rotary Clubs or the Townswomens' Guild are intimidating to all but experienced speakers, but much can be done by all levels of staff by more informal contacts; a discussion in a youth club or Sunday School might well be better received if led by a library assistant rather than an older professional member of staff.

Publicity from central sources can be used to back up local material. The recent Library Association leaflet (Figure 7.1) could be used as an indication of the range of services provided with local details added. In larger library systems there may well be a centralized production of promotional material that can take a main role in a presentation, with local staff being available to discuss points afterwards rather than introduce their own material nervously − the Sheffield City Libraries' video *Books and beyond* for instance is an excellent summary and introduction, and local staff can feel proud of what they are showing and can offer a good presentation with small effort from themselves.

In specialized libraries and information departments, every opportunity should be taken to publicize the service through the agencies or local government departments that are linked with the service. A collection of material on coping with old age, for example, might be best publicized by notices or leaflets displayed in a local DHSS office, day centres, Age Concern office, WRVS centre, and doctors' surgeries. It is to be hoped that these organizations would be fully aware of the library's

YOUR LIBRARY NEEDS YOU!

For over a century Britain has enjoyed the best public library service in the world—but that may not last much longer

★ Your local branch may be closed down.

★ It may be open only a few days a week, at a time when you can't get there.

★ The money for new books, cassettes, records, videos, may be drastically cut.

WHY?

Public libraries cost surprisingly little: about 14p per person per week—half a bar of chocolate or a daily newspaper. That's all it costs for the wealth of books, entertainment and information your library gives you.

But today some local authorities are refusing to spend even such small amounts to maintain the service. And although national government is legally responsible for making sure that a good service is provided, no one in Whitehall wants to put pressure on local councils for fear of being asked to pay more towards it.

That means it's up to YOU to get across to your elected representatives that, whatever they think, YOU think your library is important and well worth its modest cost.

Fig. 7.1

activities and would assist by mentioning the collection, and directing possible users towards it.

Contacts with local radio and local newspapers are also productive. Newspapers are often very pleased to support enthusiastically promoted events, and will interview staff and photograph premises – not intimidating activities for the participants. Local radio interviews can be more demanding, but an extrovert member of staff will enjoy the opportunity, and it is perhaps 'easier' than a direct presentation to an audience.

Public events which attract media attention are also a good opportunity for publicity of the service. Often these occasions will need the enthusiasm and effort of the younger staff members: local fairs and carnivals are a suitable chance for a library stand or float, and other parades, competitions or sporting events may appreciate support from interested organizations prepared to take part, who can thereby advertise their own service. An attractive mobile library is a good base for such activities, and can carry interesting displays and demonstrations of services as well as being a noticeable 'presence'.

Public relations will encourage use of a library service; readers' advisory work should be highlighted as an area of library work that is essentially active, rather than passive provision of a basic service. The general atmosphere of the library will further promote success: it is important obviously to decide exactly what is being promoted and to be sure that it is good. Less happy aspects of work should be sorted out before they are publicized. Many small points also contribute to the overall picture: staff manner on the telephone or in handling correspondence can have a great effect on the recipient. It is particularly difficult to be friendly or personal if standard pro-forma letters are in use. When things go wrong, it is essential to put them right with the minimum of delay; a disgruntled user, whether justified or not, is a poor advertisement, and staff at all levels need to take care that a problem patron is handled skilfully. A system of immediate referral of complaints to an experienced supervisor or manager is preferable to less experienced staff becoming involved in arguments.

To summarize, public relations is a means of encouraging use of a library service, including readers' advisory work. It involves cultivating institutional and individual contacts with users and with potential users, and also with the organization that provides funds — the school, college, local council, or information/ advice service. The goodwill that is generated will help in the development of an increasingly successful service in which more ambitious readers' advisory services will be sought and provided.

Public relations also covers relations with other staff in the service: it is important in any publicity exercise to be certain that all participants are enthusiastic and persuaded of the value of what is being done. New users will be immediately discouraged if the helpful message to which they have responded is not supported by the staff they meet on the premises.

Library publications

Official publications from the library service can also offer an opportunity for publicity: most services will need to produce an annual report to their controlling bodies, and such a document should be as attractive as possible. It would be useful to offer a balanced view of the service, pointing out the problems and constraints, but as far as possible emphasizing positive qualities and highlighting achievements over the year. The annual report should contain details of all aspects of the service, together with information on contacts and locations for different functions, and should be distributed to other library services and organizations which have a relationship with the library. Many universities and some public libraries produce a very high quality printed annual report which makes a good impression on institutional users or sponsors.

At a more local level, and more immediately relevant to readers' advisory work, a library guide is an essential publication. There is a case for the production of such a guide on an individual basis by every service point however small, even where a parent organization already produces an overall introduction. Clearly in a school or college library, or an information department, the library will need to produce its own publication, perhaps with advice and help from an art faculty member, and possibly subject to the scrutiny of the parent body. In a public library, readers prefer to know what their own service point has to offer, and whilst it is essential to point out the full range of services offered by the system, the majority of users will visit only their one 'home' branch and a specific guide to that will be valuable.

A basic library guide needs to be planned at a simple level: the inclusion of too much information will deter readers from scanning through it. The best policy is to make a brief list of the points that staff feel should be included. These might comprise:

- the address and telephone number
- details of opening hours
- the names and job titles of the staff
- details on how to join the library
- a brief description of how the stock is arranged (kept as simple as can be) mentioning all types of material in stock
- a note on other services offered at the library – community information or storytimes, perhaps
- an encouragement to readers to ask the staff to help them in finding books or seeking information
- any essential rules, which should be stated positively and with an explanation ('returning books promptly helps us to provide a wider selection of stock for all borrowers' rather than a straight instruction 'books must be returned by the due date').

It is difficult for library staff to imagine what the library seems like to a new user; often the newest members of staff may have the clearest idea of the problems. The guide should obviously be written with the level of the clientele in mind – primary schoolchildren or college students will need different information, presented appropriately. When a draft of the guide is ready, asking 'friendly' users for their comments will help sort out difficulties; it is easy to omit obvious points because they seem too obvious to the staff.

Any guide must be designed as well as the staff can manage; use an uncluttered layout with short, easily-legible pieces of text. Use only clear, simple language and avoid library jargon – 'overdues' and 'reservations' are not terms which users immediately understand.

Depending on the abilities of staff and the type of users, illustrations or cartoons may be helpful. The finished product should be typed or printed and duplicated to the best standard possible on the budget. A clear title on the front and use of a distinctive coloured paper will help to identify it. The guide should be handed out to all new users, and made freely and obviously available at several points in the library.

Depending on the type of organization and its complexity, additional material may be necessary: a guide to the catalogue and classification scheme may be essential in a secondary school or college library. Descriptions of special services available will need to be prepared in some public library service points (Figure 7.2) and in information departments. Where facilities are available, a video introduction shown to all new patrons can be an attractive proposition, but this will still need to be backed up by a leaflet that can be taken away and referred to later.

The care taken over the guide indicates to users what they can expect of the service as a whole; an attractive, readable guide will welcome patrons, and encourage them to approach staff for help. This is the vital first step towards a successful readers' advisory service.

Specific publicity activities

A further way of offering readers an advisory service is to bring to their attention areas of stock or types of service that might be of interest to them. Advantage should be taken of any national or regional opportunity to publicize the library — perhaps during a book-week, or a literacy scheme promotion, or a local literary festival.

To coincide with such events a library can sponsor a meeting, or run a competition, offer tours of the premises if this is feasible, and generally make itself available as a base for activities.

More generally, regular library-run events can generate local interest: storytimes for young children are a popular theme, and result in making children and their parents aware of the services available.

A programme of displays is a good means of stimulating interest, attracting media attention, and extending the awareness of the library's stock and services. Amateurish efforts often deter rather than attract, so care is needed to prepare materials successfully. Where no specialized assistance is available the most practical policy is to keep displays smart and simple. Use of bright, coloured paper backgrounds and large transfer or adhesive lettering will be the minimum requirements. Such materials can be locally purchased at low cost from the petty cash if there is no budget provision. A very simple and straightforward layout will be more successful unless a member of staff has a talent for graphic work.

Displays should incorporate photographs or objects if possible — library users may well volunteer to lend suitable items, or a local museum or society may be delighted to help. If there is a schedule of forthcoming displays users will have an opportunity to offer assistance well in advance. Unless the library has an

BLACK PRINT AND BLACK SOUND AT HUDDERSFIELD LIBRARY

A collection of books, cassettes and magazines is now available to all library users interested in the West Indies and Africa.

You can borrow books at no charge from the Lending Library on such subjects as poetry, religion, plays, food, history, geography, travel, music arts and crafts, politics, sport, folk beliefs, customs as well as stories and biographies by black authors.

Magazines – The Caribbean Times, Roots, Frontline and West Indian World can be read in the Reference Library.

Records by Bob Marley, Jimmy Cliff, Gregory Isaacs Eddy Grant and many more can be borrowed from the Music Library at a charge of 20p for four weeks. Some of these are on cassette as well.

We hope that this collection will help you to use the library for leisure, education and information.

KIRKLEES LIBRARIES

Fig. 7.2

enthusiasm and skill in display work it may be more valuable for readers to see a small number of well prepared displays in preference to a constant stream of indifferent attempts. No display should be left in place for more than the duration of the normal loan period.

Generally the location of a display will be a case or table on the library premises, preferably in a focal position. If displays are well presented, it will probably be possible to persuade local shops, banks or building society offices to accept a small display to be mounted on their premises; this will bring the library to the attention of a range of people who may not visit the library. Great care is needed as displays normally presented in such places, as with travel agents or sports shops, are professionally assembled.

Co-operative display programmes between different information organizations or a group of libraries can offer a good return on the initial effort of compilation and transport between sites. You need to feel confident that other people's work is of an acceptable standard, and they will have the same expectations of you.

Topics for displays are not difficult to conceive; in school or college libraries, a new topic on the curriculum will be an obvious choice, and staff may request displays for various purposes. In a more general library context topics may revolve around items of local interest, events or social considerations. National or international news, commemorations or national events may also be useful stimuli. Seasonal topics or hobbies — gardening, tennis, cricket — can be used, as can general themes, for instance 'France' which might bring together items scattered about the library in different locations — maps, guides, cookery books, wine atlases, language tapes, French literature in translation, music and recordings of French composers. Recent items of stock can be highlighted, perhaps by topic or even individual items — a new local map, an encyclopedia or general reference tool such as the *Guinness Book of Records*. Other aspects of the library's service can also be advertised: a feature on the housebound service, or a new video loan service.

Staff need to be prepared for the service 'problems' that will be caused by displays. Interest will mean increased demand: do not publicize the housebound service unless you can cope with additional requests for visits. Highlight topics in which your stock is strong; a display either locks up your stock and readers

will have to reserve items to see after the end of the display period
— frustrating, and sometimes a long delay will result if there is
only one copy of each item — or you need to top up the display
two or three times a day. For new book displays, using the jackets
only is eye-catching and allows the items to be circulating; here
again it must be possible to support the interest generated. One
copy of an item will be quite inadequate if 20 people reserve it —
can you afford additional copies?

Library staff can also offer an advisory service to readers by
preparing booklists, either on demand, or more likely on a
regular basis in line with topics known to be popular, or
seasonal, or well represented in the stock but maybe scattered by
the classification or categorization scheme. Booklists will serve to
assist readers to find interesting material, bring to their notice
items they would otherwise probably not see, and aid the best
exploitation of the stock. All staff should try to be aware of new
book publishing, read reviews and visit local bookshops, and be
familiar with new recordings, video or software if the library
handles these formats.

For compiling fiction booklists, use of the AAL publications
Fiction Index or *Junior Fiction Index* and *Sequels* or *Junior
Sequels* will be a valuable source; titles such as 'ghost stories' or
'novels set in World War II' may be readily assembled, but the
contents of a booklist should be restricted to items easily
available from the library. Inclusion of out-of-print items may
be inadvisable. Such booklists will exaggerate demand, so you
need to be sure that all staff know how to cope with extra
enquiries and reservations. A poor delivery service after a
promotion leads to disappointment and frustration.

For non-fiction booklists (we are not dealing here with highly
specialized subject bibliographies) the library's own catalogue or
a general published bibliography, such as those of the Library
Association Public Libraries Group, will be a useful basis. In
most general contexts, it is more helpful to readers to produce a
booklist including a small number of items that can be readily
available, rather than an exhaustive list that will tend to deter
rather than entice. A non-fiction list should contain brief
annotations indicating level, content and any special features.
The information given must contain a full citation — a
minimum of author, title, publisher, date and details of where
the item is located in the library.

Lists of new books can be particularly interesting, and in a public library context may be centrally produced and include material added to the stock of special departments. This serves to demonstrate to readers the full range of stock and services available from the system as a whole, and must contain information on how to obtain these items through the local service point.

School, college and information unit staff should similarly prepare booklists for special client groups or to highlight aspects of their stock.

Chapter Eight

Staff training for readers' advisory work

Throughout this book we have been concerned to stress the importance of good staff attitudes and practices to encourage successful conversations with readers. Regardless of the strengths and weaknesses of the services provided, it is true in any organization dealing with customers that the 'public face' of the system is the keystone of the public's perception of that organization.

In libraries of all types the distinction between librarians and library assistants is nowadays blurred; the distinction has in any case never been apparent to users in general who usually refer to all staff as 'librarians'. The present blurred image is due to the less rigid demarcation of jobs. Many small libraries are in the charge of non-professional supervisory staff, while qualified staff in small organizations need to do all sorts of jobs — clerical and manual as well as 'professional'.

It is important that qualified staff should be visible to the public; keeping the people supposedly most able to offer help to readers out of sight is a strange policy. It will be helpful, where the library has more than one member of staff, to split the counter area from the enquiry point. This will allow the enquiry staff to concentrate on their function and not become entangled in the issue system; the counter staff can refer problems and questions immediately to the enquiry point without breaking off from dealing with other borrowers. The staff involved in both services will probably be the same: qualified or experienced staff might spend more time on the enquiry point, but it is valuable for all assistants to become acquainted with readers' advisory work in a real situation, with more experienced staff available to help. In most small organizations everybody will need to be prepared to do everything, so that confining certain staff to one function only is unrealistic.

In very small libraries or information units the volume of routine business might be small, and the division of functions will seem impractical or irrelevant. It is still a good idea to bring to public notice that an enquiry service is available, and every opportunity should be taken to point out that staff should be approached for help. In practice, users will prefer to deal with one 'friendly' person regardless of what function is indicated: they will return books, talk about the weather, and ask a question at the same point, and the more ready the person on the other side of the counter is to help, the more conversations will take place there. Another member of staff sitting at an enquiry point a few feet away needs to be able to join in and offer support to colleagues: if the enquiry staff seem to be reluctant to be disturbed, they will be only seldom troubled and they may suggest that lack of business indicates they could move to a backroom. This would be fundamentally to misunderstand what readers' advisory work is all about. So frequently, questions from readers are not formal, composed ideas; they are niggling little problems that people would like to talk over if somebody seems prepared to listen.

A friendly, interested staff member will encourage readers to chat and put questions: for training purposes the skills of personal communication are a priority — knowledge of how to answer questions and which sources to check will only be of academic interest if users do not feel sufficiently relaxed to ask questions at all.

So, all members of staff will find themselves engaged in readers' advisory work. All members of staff should therefore receive encouragement and relevant training. Training is sometimes seen as an 'extra' activity: something done only by the organization's personnel department, something time-consuming and expensive that cannot be justifiably afforded. This attitude is ridiculous.

Everything that happens in any library, all day long, is training through experience. Readers' advisory work is a practical skill, and the training needed is practical also. Most of it can be done on the premises, however small the service and limited its resources, and requires no expense.

At a minimum it involves staff members in charge of service points writing down the training needs of the staff, including themselves. This will be a simple paper — perhaps just four or five points: how to find out what a reader really wants, basic reference books, other libraries' resources, how to deal with users. A programme needs to be drawn up for each person to cover each point over perhaps a ten-week period — half an hour per week at a quiet time. With the approval of the parent body it may be possible to close for an hour early one morning each week for training purposes, as many retail organizations do.

For training materials and methods, staff will need to liaise with a personnel department to obtain any suitable items, but more importantly to prepare their own: in a small library someone may be asked to read a chapter of a librarianship textbook — this one perhaps or something mentioned in the bibliography at the end — and write notes on their feelings about how what is recommended relates to their own service. Staff may be asked to examine a reference book, look at the contents page and index, list the topics that it covers and what sort of questions it would be useful for answering.

It is always essential in training to evaluate what has been done: all the staff should get together regularly and pool what they have learnt, and suggest what else they feel they would like to know. Their comments should form the basis of the next ten-week period, as training is a permanent, never-ending feature of the routine of the library however modest. Instead of having staff find out about their work in a haphazard way from things they happen to notice or overhear, perhaps incorrectly, we are merely sorting out what is really important and assembling materials to present this as a structured, memorable way.

At this level the costs are minimal: staff time is the only constraint. Those who would scoff here should consider that if an activity is a priority, there is time for it — it could replace shelf-tidying on one morning a week, or be seen as an extension to a coffee-break on a quiet occasion. But ideally the notice 'closed for staff training 9.00-9.30 every Thursday' provides a clear space, and puts the small amount of time into perspective.

The more difficult area for training purposes is how to deal with users — not how to find out their needs through the 'reference interview', but more generally how to handle people in any public service context. This training for interpersonal skills is not easy to carry out unaided, although there are helpful textbooks; it is best done through more advanced training techniques that need experienced guidance.

Some initial aspects can be organized without delay: interaction of staff and users by telephone is one area where progress can be readily made. Where you cannot see the person with whom you are dealing, it is more necessary to put all your 'politeness' into your voice. You cannot smile into a telephone, so you will need to use welcoming phrases: 'good morning', 'can I help you?' 'would you wait a moment, please' — the alternatives 'hello' and 'hang-on' are plain rude in most contexts, and you will find in contacting organizations by telephone, perhaps for the community information collection, that your opinion of your contact is entirely coloured by their promptness and pleasantness. If they seem curt and abrupt — and they may not intend to be — you will feel resentful and critical. Being asked to hold the line for just half a minute can seem an eternity: if it is not possible to deal with a reader quickly, offer to ring back.

Face-to-face work with readers involves all aspects of your personality; some staff find it easy and natural to deal with people, others need help and guidance, and there are techniques and training that can achieve this. 'Politeness' is the key to the whole business, but this is hard to define and such a vague term is unhelpful. Shop assistants (and library assistants) who may be very good at customer relations may see nothing wrong with continuing a conversation amongst themselves while dealing with a customer, but this is one feature of interpersonal work that causes great resentment on the part of the public — they feel subordinate to the assistants' chief interest.

Peter Jordan (1986) provides an excellent summary of training techniques appropriate to working with users; in particular he quotes a document used at Manchester Polytechnic to summarize points raised in discussion (Appendix 8.1). A supervisor in a small library might do worse than start training by talking about each of these points with staff members, and asking them to think of unsatisfactory experiences they have had in shops or banks or public transport where they have been the users. Such discussions can then draw conclusions to improve their awareness of the impact they can have on users.

As well as explaining some relevant techniques, Jordan also includes a useful bibliography of general items that could be used as background and in discussion.

Staff in very small libraries or information units, particularly if they work alone, have a problem in training terms. Self-training is only of limited value, especially in an area where interpersonal skills are being considered. For staff in this position, some outside help is essential: meetings held locally by the Library Association or its groups could be a useful basis for talking to others with similar difficulties. The Association of Assistant Librarians holds courses aimed at junior professional staff, that could be quite appropriate for experienced library assistants, and that deal with topics of general relevance. The School Library Association and Youth Libraries Group are similarly active. In urban areas, local training co-operatives are becoming a more popular means of pooling resources to good effect, and such arrangements are of especial value to small libraries.

Encouraging staff to take courses will also help to raise their self-esteem and make them more aware of their performance and abilities; a local college may run the library-related modules of BTEC courses, or the City and Guilds Library and Information Assistants' Certificate. Staff who attend such courses should be asked to talk about their experiences, and discuss the relevance of what they are doing at a regular training session/staff meeting even in the smallest service point.

Readers' advisory work is heavily dependent on staff and users talking face to face; in an introductory volume we can only deal with the most basic points, and where a library system is running more comprehensive training schemes, these ideas may seem very modest. However, even the simplest training can have a marked effect, and if staff can be made aware of some of the pitfalls, progress can be made to avoid them. Training also makes staff feel that their employer is interested in them and the effect of the job they are doing: simply running any training has a positive effect on motivation, and over a longer term will result in a more able and effective workforce.

Appendix 8.1   Interpersonal skills and service to users

Key points to be brought out in discussion
1 Serving the user has priority over everything else. Staff should try to put themselves in the user's position and imagine his/her feelings and reactions.
2 Staff should always be polite and helpful and should avoid losing their 'cool' even if provoked.
3 Staff should not pretend they know if they do not.

4   Queries should be passed on to others who do know the answers. Assistants should know when queries should be passed on to professional staff.
5   Users should not be left standing for long periods not knowing what is happening to their query.
6   Conflict situations should be moved away from busy counter areas as far as possible.
7   Users should be treated consistently according to the library's rules and policies even though assistants may be tempted to make exceptions.
8   Counters and desks should, as far as possible, not be left unattended while assistants disappear to sort out queries.
9   Messages for others should be understood and passed on accurately and legibly. Information should include time, date, and name of recipient.
10 Users should not be 'fobbed off' and assistants should ensure they have done nothing to prevent the queries being taken seriously.
11 Assistants should not discuss users in public.
12 Users should not be 'ordered' to do things in a terse fashion.

[Manchester Polytechnic Library]

Chapter Nine

Conclusion

This volume has attempted to show that readers' advisory work is a pervasive activity in libraries and information units. We have deliberately concentrated on the basics of the subject, and have therefore assumed an audience in smaller libraries — schools, colleges, public branches and mobile services — and in specialized information services. Staff in such organizations will be few in number, and a rigid demarcation into professional and non-professional duties is unlikely to be feasible. In readers' advisory work, all staff have an important role to play, whether qualified or unqualified, experienced or inexperienced.

It is not possible to categorize readers' advisory work as an independent activity, confined to certain staff, or certain hours of the week, or certain premises only; all contact between staff and users has the potential to develop into enquiry work. The simplest questions need to be carefully handled to encourage users to make fuller use of their library service; simple questions are more likely to be addressed to an assistant working at a lending counter or shelving books. It is in this informal way that the majority of users will prefer to approach the staff; a 'formal' arrangement to speak to a 'readers' advisor' will deter more than encourage. Larger-scale, extensive enquiries clearly need expert handling and are beyond the scope of an introductory book.

Most aspects of public work in a library or information department will be covered by our definition of readers' advisory work: it begins outside the library with awareness of the service, advertising of what is available, continues into the accessibility and appeal of premises and environment, and then embraces passive methods of assistance — successful guiding and attractive introductory materials.

The core of our material has been a discussion of how to

handle all types of simple enquiries — bibliographical, reference, fiction — and we have suggested basic source material that any small service might possess. However, it is important to relate the stock and services of any library or information unit very closely to the needs of its patrons; we have therefore seen readers' advisory work as including a basic understanding of what the clientele group comprises, and how to find out readers' needs. Consequently we have discussed community information in our survey, as the finding, organizing and exploitation of such a collection will be of direct help to users and thus a legitimate part of readers' advisory work.

The key to success in this subject is staff attitudes: it is over-idealistic to hope for all staff to be involved, committed, and knowledgeable, but quite sensible to encourage a positive, helpful attitude in everyone. This can be fostered by simple methods of training and the immediate results may be impressive; many other 'public' organizations in competitive situations — banks, building societies, department stores, hotels — know the value of a helpful image put across by any member of staff a user might meet or talk to. The gulf between organizations which train their staff to be helpful and those that do not can be very noticeable; if a major part of our role is to help people, we cannot afford to be in the second category.

Relating to user needs, and the application of simple training are the two themes which emerge everywhere from these pages; whilst both these can be highly developed, this book deals with basic points, and the simple nature of our discussion should be seen as just an introduction to the subject.

There has been very little written material on readers' advisory work in recent years; what there is has usually been included in more general works, and thus makes less impact. The bibliography which follows contains several basic textbooks which further develop the idea of readers' advisory work in various library and information contexts; chapters in each of the cited works will provide fuller information on user needs, more ideas on what sort of activities to pursue, and advice on how to promote and encourage the training of staff for this most central area of information and library work.

Bibliography

Bakewell, K.G.B., *Business information in the public library,* Aldershot, Gower Publishing, 1987.

Bunch, A., *Basics of information work,* London, Bingley, 1984.

Bunch, A., *Community information services,* London, Bingley, 1982.

Chirgwin, F.J. and Oldfield, P., *Library assistant's manual,* 2nd ed., London, Bingley, 1982. 3rd ed. to be published 1988.

Collison, R.L., *Library assistance to readers,* 5th ed., London, Crosby Lockwood, 1965.

Fjallbrant, N. and Malley, I., *User education in libraries,* London, Bingley, 1984.

Grogan, D., *Practical reference work,* London, Bingley, 1979.

Harrison, C. and Beenham, R., *Basics of librarianship,* 2nd ed., London, Bingley, 1985.

Harrison, K.C., *Public relations for librarians,* 2nd ed., Aldershot, Gower Publishing, 1982.

Hepworth, P., *Primer of assistance to readers,* London, Association of Assistant Librarians, 1951.

Herring, J.E., *School librarianship,* London, Bingley, 1982. 2nd ed. to be published 1988.

Hicken, M., (1986) 'Stock management', in *Handbook of library training practice,* R.J. Prytherch (ed.), Aldershot, Gower Publishing, 1986.

Hicken, M. and Kaye, R., 'Training in community librarianship', in *Handbook of library training practice.* R.J. Prytherch (ed.), Aldershot, Gower Publishing, 1986.

Jackaman, P., *Basic reference and information work,* Huntingdon, Elm Publications, 1985.

Jordan, P., 'Training in handling users', in *Handbook of library training practice*, R.J. Prytherch (ed.), Aldershot, Gower Publishing, 1986.

Katz, W., *Your library : a reference guide*, 2nd ed., New York, Holt, Rinehart & Winston, 1984.

Library Association Working Party on Training, *Training in libraries*, London, Library Association, 1977.

Malley, I., *Basics of information skills teaching*, London, Bingley, 1984.

Sherman, S., *ABC's of library promotion*, Metuchen NJ, Scarecrow Press, 1971.

Stanley, S., 'Information sources', in *Handbook of library training practice*, R.J. Prytherch (ed.), Aldershot, Gower Publishing, 1986.

Turner, C., *Organizing information: principles and practice*, London, Bingley, 1987.

Webb, S., *Creating an information service*, London, Aslib, 1983.

Index

Entries in bold type refer to figures and appendices